Ed… oe

Adaptat… …tivities by Kenneth Brodey

Illustrated by Gianni De Conno

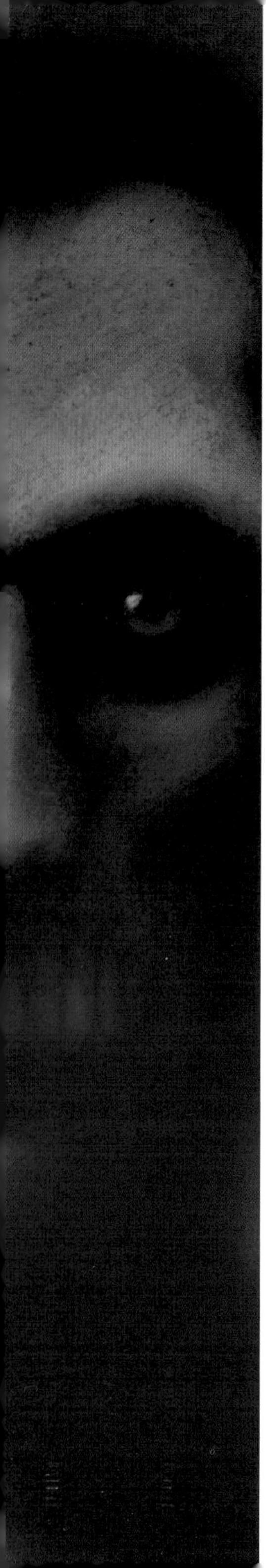

Editor: Michela Bruzzo
Design and art direction: Nadia Maestri
Computer graphics: Carla Devoto, Simona Corniola
Picture research: Laura Lagomarsino

First edition: January 2010

Picture credits
Library of Congress, Prints and Photographs Division, Washington: 4; ROADSHOW FILM LIMITED / Album: 27; © Bettmann / Corbis: 28; De Agostini Picture Library: 67, 69, 79 bottom left, 80, 84 left, 84 centre right, 106; Webphoto: 68

We would be happy to receive your comments and suggestions, and give you any other information concerning our material.
info@blackcat-cideb.com
www.blackcat-cideb.com

ISBN 978-88-530-1022-3 Book + CD

Printed in Italy by Litoprint, Genoa

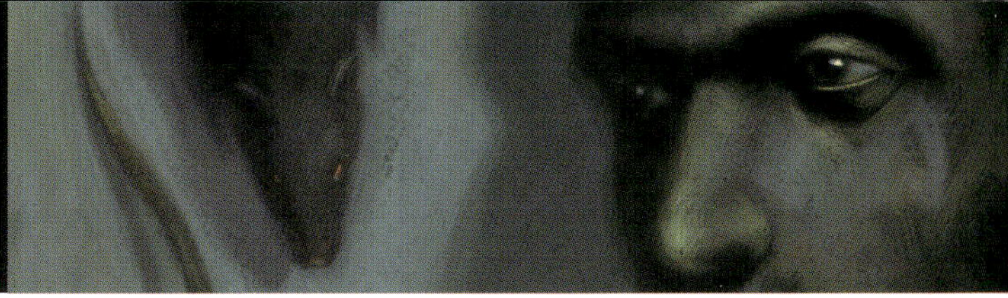

Contents

These symbols indicate the beginning and end of the passages linked to the listening activities.

Edgar Allan Poe

About the Author

Edgar Allan Poe is famous for his tales of horror. He is also considered the inventor of the modern detective story, the modern short story itself and modernist poetry. In addition he was one of the earliest creators of science fiction.

He was born on 19 January, 1809 in Boston. His parents were both actors. When Edgar was only two years old his father left the family. His mother died on 8 December, 1811. Fortunately, Mrs. Frances Allan, the wife of John Allan, a businessman from Richmond, Virginia, heard about the Poe children. As an act of charity she decided to bring Edgar to live in her house. She was impressed with his good looks. In 1815 the Allans, together with Edgar, went to live in England for five years. When they returned to the United States in 1820 Edgar went to private schools in Richmond. In 1826 he went to the University of Virginia. He was a very good student.

In 1827 he published his first book of poems. In 1833 Edgar won a literary contest for his short story "MS. Found in a Bottle" [1]. This was the beginning of Edgar's professional career as a writer.

From 1835 to 1837 he worked as the editor of the literary magazine the *Southern Literary Messenger*. He did an extremely good job: sales increased from 500 to 3,500 copies. In 1836 he married his cousin Virginia Clemm. Like Edgar's mother, she had tuberculosis [2], and for the next ten years until her death she was constantly ill.

Even with Edgar's success as an editor he didn't make enough money to support his family. He therefore moved to New York and then to Philadelphia in 1838 and then back to New York in 1844, always looking for better jobs.

In 1840 he published his greatest tales in a collection called *Tales of the Grotesque* and Arabesque. In 1843 he wrote "The Gold Bug", a kind of treasure hunt story with hidden clues, which sold 300,000 copies. This story brought Poe fame, but not financial security. In fact he often worked 15 hours a day, and still he did not have enough money to feed his family.

In 1845 Edgar's most famous poem, "The Raven", was published. He was finally famous. But in 1847 his wife died. This "intolerable sorrow" caused Edgar to drink. He returned to Richmond in 1849. On October 3, 1849 Edgar was found unconscious in front of a voting station in Baltimore. He was taken to hospital, where he died four days later.

1. **MS.** : Manuscript.
2. **tubercolosis** : serious infectious desease that affects someone's lungs.

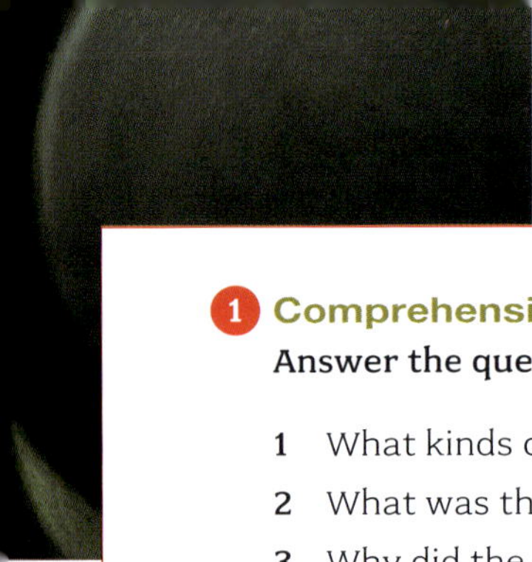

1 Comprehension check

Answer the questions about Edgar Allan Poe's life.

1 What kinds of literature did Poe create?
2 What was the profession of Poe's parents?
3 Why did the Allan family decide to have Poe live with them?
4 Where did Poe study?
5 How old was Poe when he began his literary career?
6 What did Poe do for the *Southern Literary Messenger*?
7 Why did Poe continue to move from city to city?
8 Who did Poe marry?
9 Describe Poe's story "The Gold Bug".
10 What is the name of Poe's most famous poem?

INTERNET PROJECT

More about Poe

To find out more about Edgar Allan Poe's life connect to the Internet and go to www.blackcat-cideb.com. Insert the title or part of the title of the book into our search engine.
Open the page for *American Horror*. Click on the Internet project links.
With your partner find out some more interesting facts about

- Poe's life
- Poe's school
- Poe's death
- Poe's city
- Poe's stories: science-fiction, detective stories and short stories

Present what you have found to the class.

The Pit and the Pendulum

Before you read

1 What is frightening?

Poe wrote "The Pit and the Pendulum" in the style of stories printed by the famous *Blackwood's Magazine*. These stories present a person in a dangerous situation. The person describes in detail his feelings and sensations. One man, for example, describes how he was trapped under a giant bell in the tower of church.

Look at the list of possible situations below. With your partner put them in order from the most frightening to the least frightening.

- You are crushed by burning hot iron panels
- You are slowly cut in half by a giant knife.
- You are buried alive in a tomb.
- You are pushed into a deep dark hole.
- You are closed in a cellar full of insects, spiders and rats.

2 Vocabulary

Match the pictures to the words below. Use a dictionary to help you.

1 pitcher	3 scythe	5 dungeon
2 loaf of bread	4 gears	6 pit

A

B

C

D

E

F

3 Listening

FCE

Listen to the first part of the story. You will hear about a man who is condemned to death. For questions 1-6, choose the correct answer — A, B or C.

1 The last things the man saw before he lost consciousness were

A ☐ some candles.

B ☐ the faces of six monks.

C ☐ darkness and a bright light.

2 Some men carried him

A ☐ to a room with candles.

B ☐ up to a dark room.

C ☐ down into the darkness.

3 They finally arrived where

A ☐ he felt heat and dampness.

B ☐ he heard strange sounds.

C ☐ he heard nothing and felt dampness.

4 The first thing he heard when he woke up again was

A ☐ his own pocket watch.

B ☐ his own heart.

C ☐ his hands hitting each other.

5 The man did not have the courage to

A ☐ stand up.

B ☐ open his eyes.

C ☐ consider his situation.

6 When he opened his eyes he saw

A ☐ candle light and darkness.

B ☐ just complete darkness.

C ☐ a strange light and darkness.

I was sick from the terrible suffering. Then, finally, the judges of the Spanish Inquisition [1] gave their sentence. I was condemned to death. I looked at the seven white candles on the table, and then I lost consciousness.

After this I remember that some tall men picked me up and began to carry me. They took me down and down and down – my descent seemed unending. Finally, we came to a point where all was still and quiet and damp.

Sound and motion returned. I became aware of my heart inside of me, and I heard the sound of its beating. I lay without thinking for a long time. Then, very suddenly, I began to think,

1. **Spanish Inquisition** : (1478-1834) A law court of the Roman Catholic Church established to punish heretics—people who had other religious beliefs.

and I became horribly afraid. I wanted to know where I was and what my condition was.

So far I had not opened my eyes. I felt that I lay on my back and that I was not tied up. I wanted to open my eyes and look around, but I did not have the courage.

Finally I opened my eyes and all around me was the blackness of eternal night. I had trouble breathing. I tried to reason in order to understand my situation.

First, I was certain that I was not dead. I knew that the Spanish Inquisition used the auto-da-fés [2] to carry out its death sentences. They had had one the night before my trial. Perhaps they had sent me back to the dungeon [3] to wait a number of months for another one. But this was not the situation because in that moment the Spanish Inquisition needed new victims. Also, the cells of the dungeons in Toledo [4] all had some light.

Then I had a frightening idea and I fainted again. When I recovered, I moved my arms about wildly. I felt nothing. But I did not walk because I was terrified that I was in a tomb. Finally I began to walk. Fortunately, at least, I was not buried alive – the worst fate of all. Still, I knew that something horrible awaited me. Perhaps they were going to leave me here to die of starvation.

Then, I felt what seemed to be a wall. It was very smooth, damp and slippery. [5] I decided to measure the distance around my dungeon. But it was dark. I was going to take a knife out of

2. **auto-da-fés** : Portuguese for "act of faith": this was the public execution of a heretic—usually by burning.
3. **dungeon** : an underground prison in a castle.
4. **Toledo** : Spanish city that became the center of the Inquisition.
5. **slippery** : wet and difficult to walk on or to hold.

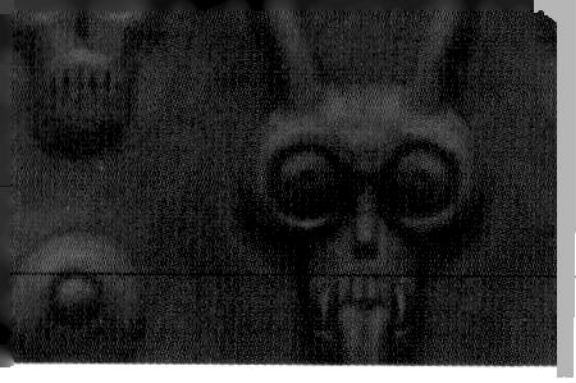

my pocket and place it in the wall. This way I would know where I started walking from. But they had taken my clothing, and now I wore a long wool shirt. For a long time I did not know what to do. I was totally confused. Then I decided to tear off[6] a piece of the edge of my long shirt, and lay the piece again the wall.

I started to walk. But the floor was very slippery, the dungeon seemed very big and I was very tired. I succeeded in walking with great effort, and I tripped[7] and fell. I was so tired that I slept for some time.

When I awoke, I felt around in the total darkness with my hand and discovered a loaf of bread and a pitcher of water. I ate and drank immediately. Then I got up and walked around, and finally I reached the piece of shirt. Before I fell I had counted 52 steps and then after I started again I counted 48 more. I reckoned that there were two steps in a yard,[8] and so the distance around the entire dungeon was 50 yards.

I had no object in my research. I certainly did not hope to find a way out of this dark dungeon. A vague curiosity pushed me. I then left the wall and decided to cross the floor. As I walked, the torn part of my shirt got tangled between my legs and I fell face down on the floor. I was rather confused after the fall and at first I did not notice something unusual: my chin was on the floor of the dungeon, but my lips and the top part of my head were lower than my chin and touched nothing. Then I felt cold moist air coming up against my forehead. I put forward my arms and was terrified to discover that I had fallen to the edge of a circular

6. **tear off** : pull into pieces.
7. **tripped** : knocked his foot against something.
8. **yard** : a unit of length equal to 91.9 centimetres or 36 inches.

pit. I felt with my hand on the wall of this pit and pulled off a piece of stone. I dropped the stone and listened. It bounced against the sides of the pit for many seconds and finally I heard the sound as it hit some water at the bottom. Then, above me, I heard the sound of the quick opening and closing of a door, while a light flashed in the darkness for a second.

I realized the horrible fate I had avoided. There were two kinds of torture – physical and psychological. I, it seemed, had to suffer the second kind. Now every part of my body was shaking from fear. I moved slowly back to the wall, away from the pit. My fear was so great that I stayed awake for many hours. At last, I fell asleep.

When I awoke, again I found a pitcher of water and a loaf. I was very thirsty and I drank all the water. I think there was a drug in the water because I soon slept very deeply. I do not know how long I slept but when I woke there was light in the dungeon and I could see.

One of the first things I noticed was its size – it was much smaller than I had thought. Its whole circumference was only about 25 yards. This bothered me greatly. How could that be? Obviously, in my horrible situation, this had very little importance. But I still desperately wanted to understand my mistake. Then I understood. After I had put down the piece of my shirt I walked slowly around the room and then I stopped and slept. At this point I had almost arrived at the piece of shirt, but when I awoke I did not go forward. Without realizing it, I had turned around and went back to the beginning again.

Now, I could also see the shape of the room. It was square and the walls were made of large iron panels. There were horrible pictures of devils and skeletons on these panels, but they were all rather blurred and faded. [9] I could also see the circular pit in the center of the dungeon.

I managed to see all this with great difficulty because I was tied to a low wooden platform by a single long leather belt. This belt formed a kind of a spiral [10] all along my body. Only my left arm was a little free, and with great effort I took some meat from a plate. But I then noticed to my horror that they had taken away the pitcher. I say to my horror because the meat was very spicy and it greatly stimulated my thirst.

I looked up and saw that the ceiling too was made of large panels of iron. Then I noticed an interesting picture on the ceiling directly over me. It was an image of Father Time, [11] but instead of holding a scythe he was holding what seemed to be the picture of a pendulum – the pendulum itself and the gears of its machinery. For some reason it attracted my attention greatly. While I looked at it, for a moment I thought it moved. Then a second later I was certain that it really did move. The pendulum was going back and forth.

9. **faded** : less bright.
10. **spiral** : a shape that winds round and round.
11. **Father Time** : a personification of time.

The text and **beyond**

1 Comprehension check

Match the phrases in column in A with those in column B. There are two phrases in column B that you do not need to use.

A

1 The narrator knew he was not in a dungeon of Toledo
2 The narrator moved his arms about
3 The narrator tore off a piece of his shirt
4 The narrator first realized there was a pit
5 The narrator pulled off a piece of stone from the wall of the pit
6 When there was finally light in the dungeon, the narrator still found it difficult to observe his prison
7 The picture of Father Time was unusual

B

A because he held a pendulum.
B because his chin was higher than his forehead.
C because he wanted to know how deep it was.
D because he wanted to know if they had buried him alive.
E because it was cold and damp.
F because he was tied down.
G because it was completely dark.
H because he wanted to measure the dungeon.
I because he heard something fall and hit its sides and then the bottom.

2 In the dark

Which of the illustrations below shows how the narrator walked in his prison, when he tried to estimate its size?

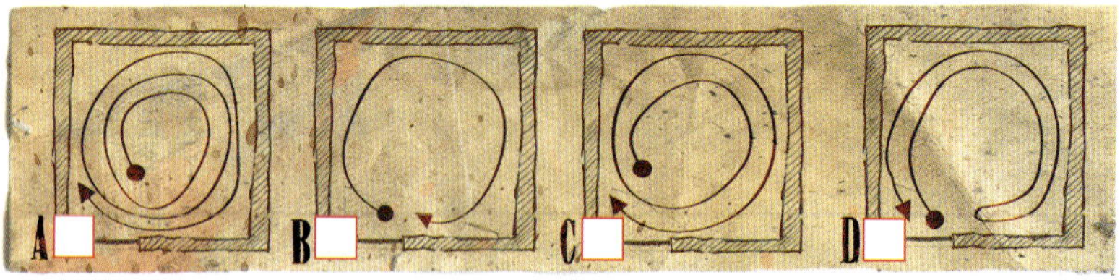

FCE 3 The Spanish Inquisition

For questions 1-10, read the text below. Use the word given in capitals at the of some of the lines to form a word that fits in the space in the same line. There is an example at the beginning (0).

The Inquisition was a tribunal, or court, set up by the Catholic Church in 1231.
The main activity of this tribunal was the (0) ..investigation.. of heretics — people who did not accept the doctrines and ideas of the Church. **INVESTIGATE**
The Inquisition had two Inquisitors, (**1**) .... and police. **ASSIST** The Inquisition was allowed to use torture to obtain (**2**) .... from those accused of heresy. **CONFESS**
This first Inquisition became increasingly (**3**) .... in the two centuries that followed until it disappeared. **IMPORTANT** Then in Spain another Inquisition was established by King Ferdinand in 1478. Its main object was to investigate the (**4**) .... beliefs **RELIGION** of Jews and Muslims who had (**5**) .... converted to Catholicism. **RECENT**
Its head or Grand Inquisitor was the infamous Tomàs de Torquemada.
Historians estimated that Torquemada had about 2,000 heretics burned. The Spanish Inquisition continued until 1834. Spanish monarchs supported it (**6**) .... **COMPLETE**
This was (**7**) .... true of Philip II, who tried to invade England in 1588. **PARTICULAR** This is why the Spanish Inquisition became part of English and Protestant propaganda against Catholic Spain. (**8**) ...., **LATE** in the late 1700s and early 1800s, English writers of Gothic novels often gave horrifying but (**9**) .... descriptions of the tortures and **FICTION** and (**10**) .... of the Inquisition. **SUFFER** Poe's pit and pendulum follow in this tradition.

Before you read

1 Prediction

What do you think is going to happen?

2 Listening

3 FCE

You will hear about some more horrors in the dungeon. For questions 1-5, choose the correct answer — A, B or C.

1 The narrator first noticed the rats when they
- A ☐ bit him.
- B ☐ ran over his leg.
- C ☐ made a sound.

2 The rats came up because they
- A ☐ were frightened by something in the pit.
- B ☐ were attracted by the light.
- C ☐ wanted to eat the narrator's food.

3 The sharp part of the pendulum was made of
- A ☐ diamonds.
- B ☐ steel.
- C ☐ gold.

4 The pendulum moved down towards the narrator
- A ☐ extremely slowly.
- B ☐ fairly slowly.
- C ☐ fairly quickly.

5 The narrator couldn't think clearly because he had been
- A ☐ afraid.
- B ☐ hungry.
- C ☐ sleepy.

I heard a noise. I looked at the floor and saw many enormous rats. They were coming out of the pit. They were attracted by the smell of the meat. It took much effort and attention to scare them away.

After about half an hour, I looked up at the ceiling. The curve of the movement of the pendulum had increased by nearly a yard. But I was particularly worried because it had also *descended.* I now observed — with horror, of course — that the bottom part of the pendulum was a crescent of bright, heavy steel. It was also clear that the bottom part of this steel was as sharp as a razor. It was attached to a heavy metal rod, [12] and the whole thing hissed [13] as it swung through the air.

12. **rod** : a long thin bar.
13. **hissed** : made sharp 'S' sound.

Why should I describe the long hours and days I lay and watched the pendulum? It swung back and forth, and slowly — very, very slowly — descended. I even prayed that it would come down quickly and kill me, and tried to push my body up closer. I became mad. Then, suddenly, I became calm, and lay smiling at the bright steel death—as a child smiles at a sparkling toy.

Then I lost consciousness again. I do not know for how long. The pendulum had not come any closer, but I knew the monks of the Inquisition could stop it when they wanted. I was extremely hungry and reached to get what had remained of the meat. Then I had part of an idea, a hope, but that disappeared in an instant. The days and days of terror had made me an idiot — I could barely think anymore. END

I could see that the pendulum would cut across my body at the level of my heart. I knew that after it first touched and began to cut my shirt that it would take several minutes to cut my shirt completely and arrive at my skin. Here my thoughts stopped. I could not continue.

Down and down it came — slowly, very slowly. It was now three inches from my chest. I took a crazy pleasure in contrasting the slow movement down with the quick movement of the swing. To the right-to the left-to the right-to the left it screamed like a spirit, and then it moved down slowly toward my heart, like a hunting tiger.

Down and down it came. I even tried to move my half-free left hand. Maybe I could grab it and stop it. Ridiculous. That would be like stopping an avalanche.[14]

14. **avalanche** : a large mass of snow.

Down – never stopping – and down it came. I opened my eyes and watched the pendulum swing up, and then when it came flying down I closed my eyes.

Then I thought about the belt that held me down. I was not tied down by anything else. If the pendulum cut through the belt, I could escape. But certainly the monks of the Inquisition had thought of this. I lifted my head and looked. I saw that the belt was not over my heart – the point where the pendulum would cut me. Then almost immediately after my head fell back down, I had that idea again – the piece of an idea I had when I ate my meat.

For many hours rats had run all over the dungeon. I had to move my hand about to keep them away from my meat. Soon they became used to the movement of my hand, and sometimes they bit me. Now I took the remaining piece of meat and rubbed it on the belt everywhere that I could. Then I stopped moving. For a moment the rats were frightened. Then a few of the more courageous ones came and sniffed the belt. This was a signal to the others, and soon I was covered with them. They were all over me. They touched my hands and my lips. Words cannot describe my disgust, but I remained still while they ate the belt. Finally, the belt broke. I moved carefully to the side. Then I was *free*.

Free and still a prisoner of the Inquisition! As soon I was off the low table, the pendulum and its machinery were pulled up to the ceiling. Of course, they were watching me, and now they had some other terrible torture waiting for me. I looked around the room. I felt some change had happened. But I couldn't understand what it was. Then I could see. The blurred and faded pictures I mentioned earlier were now becoming more and more distinct and clear. Now horrible devils and monsters stared at me from the wall, and glowed with the light of fire. I could not convince myself that they were unreal.

Unreal! I could smell heated iron! The walls became bright red from heat. I walked slowly to the round pit — its coolness seemed wonderful then. It attracted me.

The heat increased. There had been a second change in the dungeon — and now the change was obviously in the *form*. Two of the angles of the square room were now acute, [15] and two, consequently, obtuse. [16] They were pushing me into the pit. For a moment I considered throwing myself against the burning hot walls. I did not want to fall into the pit, but gradually I was forced to move closer and closer. I felt that I was about to fall—I turned my eyes away.

Then I heard many human voices, and a sound like many trumpets. Then a horrible sound like a thousand thunders. The burning walls went quickly back. An arm caught me just as I was about to fall. It was General Lasalle's [17] arm. The French army had entered Toledo. The Inquisition was in the hands of its enemies.

15. **acute** : an acute angle is less than 90°.
16. **obtuse** : an obtuse angle is between 90° to 180°.
17. **General Lasalle** (1775-1809) : was a French Cavalry General during the Revolutionary and Napoleonic Wars.

The text and **beyond**

1 Comprehension check

Say whether the following statements are true (T) or false (F), and then correct the false ones.

		T	F
1	The narrator did not have much trouble protecting his food from the rats.	☐	☐
2	The narrator pushed himself up in order to break the belt.	☐	☐
3	The narrator imagined the pendulum cutting through his skin and muscles until it killed him.	☐	☐
4	The narrator tried to block the pendulum with his hand.	☐	☐
5	For a moment, the narrator thought that maybe the pendulum would cut the belt and free him.	☐	☐
6	The rats liberated the narrator.	☐	☐
7	The narrator was certain that the monks observed his actions.	☐	☐
8	The narrator thought that monsters and devils were actually looking at him.	☐	☐
9	When he realized the walls were hot, the narrator decided to jump into the pit.	☐	☐
10	The narrator was saved by a French general.	☐	☐

2 Like a tiger

Why does Poe compare the pendulum to a tiger? Discuss this with your partner. Below are some ideas. You can use them, change them or make up your own. Report your ideas to the class.

A A tiger moves quickly and then kills its frightened prey .

B The pendulum makes a horrible, frightening noise like a hissing tiger.

C A tiger approaches its prey slowly before the final attack.

D The shiny steel of the pendulum reflects light like a tiger's eyes.

3 A strange predicament

Nobody is certain whether "The Pit and the Pendulum" is a serious story or a parody of the popular sensation stories of the day. Maybe it was both. Write your own predicament story (story about a difficult situation) in 180-200 words. Your story can be serious or humorous. Here are some ideas.

- You have drunk a strange liquid by mistake. You think it is poison. It is summer and no doctors are around.
- You get locked in your apartment on the seventh floor, and you see a fire has started on the second. The phone is broken. You have a sore throat and can't shout.
- You are locked in the large refrigerator of a restaurant on Saturday evening. The restaurant is closed on Sunday. It is summer and so you are wearing very light clothing.

Say:

- how you ended up in the terrible situation
- your feelings and sensations
- how you finally escaped

4 Summary

Number the paragraphs in the right order to make a summary of the story.

.... He tried to think of some ways to escape. First he thought that the pendulum itself would cut the belt. Then he decided to rub the belt with some meat, and let the rats eat the belt.

.... This idea worked and he escaped from the platform. But then he noticed that the walls were heated, and that they were moving towards him.

..10... His only choice was to jump into the cool pit. Fortunately, just as he was about to fall, he was saved by a French general.

.... He then decided to investigate his dark prison. He walked around the prison in the dark.
Then he tried to cross the prison but he fell down.

.... Then he also noticed a giant pendulum directly above him, and this pendulum was moving. The pendulum continued to descend slowly for days.

.... When he awoke he could finally see his prison. He also discovered that he was tied to a wooden platform by a single long belt.

.... It was then that he realized that there was a circular pit in the center of the dungeon. He went back to the walls.

...1... The narrator was condemned to death by the Spanish Inquisition. He was carried deep down to a dark dungeon. He lost consciousness.

.... Later he found some water and bread. There was probably a drug in the water because he slept for a long time.

.... When he awoke, he reasoned about his situation: Was he buried alive? Was he going to be a victim of the *auto-da-fes*?

INTERNET PROJECT

Terrifying puppets

An excellent short film was made of "The Pit and Pendulum".
To find out more about this short film connect to the Internet and go to www.blackcat-cideb.com. Insert the title or part of the title of the book into our search engine. Open the page for *American Horror*. Click on the Internet project links.
With your partner find out:

- who made it
- how it was made
- why it is particular
- awards it has won

Watch the trailer and then say whether you think your class would like it.

Scene from the film ***The Matrix*** (1999).

Poe's *scientific imagination*

Computers, the World Wide Web, the Internet, mobile phones – this is our world today. A time before these things existed (the World Wide Web was created in 1989 and was first widely used in 1993) seems like ancient history. What? A world without cell phones! Without iPods! Without Internet! For this reason, writers and filmmakers who give us their vision of the future often show us worlds dominated by thinking computers, massive systems of digitalized thought. The 1999 film *The Matrix*, for example, presented a world that was simulated by computers; in other words, our world was actually a virtual world. Judging by the huge success of this film, its sequels and the related video games, the general public had little trouble imagining such things.

In the same way, after the Soviet Union launched the first artificial satellite into space in 1957 and after the first man traveled in space in 1961, everybody's ideas of the future were dominated by space travel. Indeed, with all the space flights of the 1960s and the first

Michael Faraday's laboratory at the Royal Institute (1870).

man on the moon in 1969, it was not difficult for people to believe in the reality of travel to distant parts of the universe, as shown in the TV show *Star Trek* (1966-69); or the 1968 film *2001: A Space Odyssey*, which mixed scientific ideas about time travel and space travel.

But ours are not the only generations to be attracted by the possibilities of science. Edgar Allan Poe lived in a time when science – for the first time in history – promised to change the world completely. Modern chemistry had recently begun when Antoine Lavoisier (1743-1794) showed what happened when something burned and how the respiration of animals was related to burning. He also developed the concept of chemical elements: everything that existed was composed of these simple elements. After Newton had summed up the suns, planets and universe in mathematical formulas, Lavoisier reduced all the substances on this planet to a simple table of elements.

Then there were the great discoveries and creations involving electricity, magnetism and electromagnetism by Luigi Galvani, Alessandro Volta and Michael Faraday, to name just a few.

At the time, it seemed that scientists with their work on electricity had discovered the essence of life. Mary Shelley's 1818 novel *Frankenstein* showed a scientist using the ideas of Galvani to bring a monster to life.

Edgar Allan Poe, who was also an amateur mathematician, was fascinated by the scientific discoveries of his day. In one of his short stories, "The Thousand-and-Second Tale of Scheherazade", he celebrated all the fabulous discoveries of his day. He presented these discoveries as if they were the wonders from the collection of tales *The Thousand and One Nights*. These marvels included the telegraph, the photograph, steamships that could cross the Atlantic Ocean, the first computer (a machine that could calculate with precision up to 31 digits – developed by Charles Babbage in the 1820s), the first trains, batteries and metal threads so thin that they could only be seen with a microscope. He also celebrated the many exciting discoveries in biology, astronomy and geology: small animals that create underwater mountains (coral); wood made of stone (fossil trees, or petrified forests) and the latest estimates of the speed of light and the distance of the stars (Poe refers the fabulous fact that the light of some stars which we see in the sky comes from stars that no longer exist!)

But Poe went even further. He wrote stories that mixed

Charles Babbage's automatic computing engine.

scientific facts with imagination. Sometimes he made it seem as if these stories were actually true. His famous "The Unparalleled Adventure of One Hans Pfaall" describes in great scientific detail a trip to the moon. "The Facts in the Case of M. Valdemar" (see page 31) showed modern science stopping death. In this story, Poe gives as much scientific-like information as he can. When the story was published, many people thought it was true. He even gave a scientific version of the end of the world in his short story "The Colloquy of Monos and Una". Although France's Jules Verne (1828-1905) is generally considered the founder of modern science fiction, Verne himself acknowledged Poe as his inspiration. Poe was also one of the first writers to produce scientific versions of traditional horror stories. This mixture of dark horror and science fiction lasts to this day – the monsters and horrors of our scientific future are often quite similar to those of our legendary and mythic past.

1 Comprehension check

Answer the following questions.

1 What kind of world does the film *The Matrix* present?

2 What technological developments inspired science fiction films in the 1960s?

3 Who first developed the scientific idea of chemical elements?

4 Who described the movements of planets and stars in mathematical formulas?

5 In the novel *Frankenstein*, what does the scientist use to bring a creature to life?

6 Why does Poe call his story about scientific discoveries "The Thousand-and-Second Tale of Scheherazade"?

7 Which of the following were not yet invented in Poe's life time? Batteries, computers, radios, trains, photography or the telegraph?

The Facts in the Case of M. Valdemar

Before you read

1 Reading pictures

Look at these photographs.
The man in the first picture is Sir Edmund Hillary, a famous explorer. The man in the second picture is Kenneth A. Arnold, an American businessman and pilot. Both men are showing pictures of things that they say are real.
Discuss the following questions with your partner, and then report your ideas to the class.

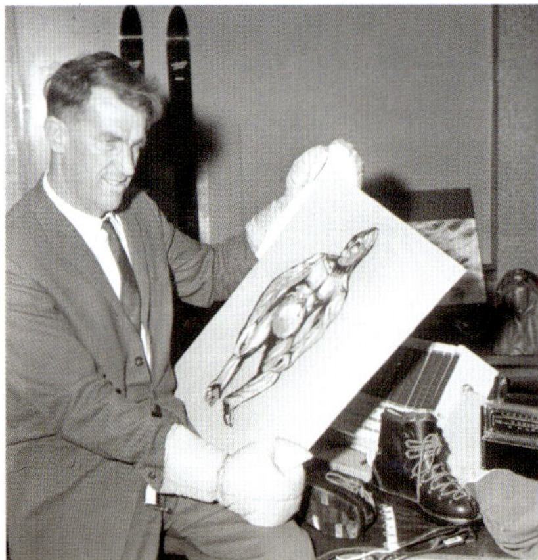

- What are the two pictures of?
- Do you think the men are lying or telling the truth?
- If they are lying, why do you think they are lying?
- Do you believe in the things in the pictures?
- Why do you think magazines, newspapers and the TV talk about these things?
- Look up the word "hoax" in your dictionary. Does it describe these two pictures?

Roswell Daily Record

RAAF Captures Flying Sauc
On Ranch in Roswell Regic

Claims Army Is Stacking Courts Martial

House Passes Tax Slash by Large Margin

Security Council Paves Way to Talks On Arms Reductions

No Details of Flying Disk Are Revealed

Ex-King Carol Weds Mme. Lupesc

Some of Soviet Satellites May Attend Paris Meeting

Roswellians Have Differing Opinions On Flying Saucers

American League Wins All-Star Game

Miners and Operators Highest Wage Pact in

The picture at the bottom shows the front page of a real newspaper that was published on 8 July, 1947 in the town of Roswell, New Mexico. RAAF stands for Roswell Army Air Field.

- Do you think the people who wrote the article and published it really believed the story?
- If they didn't believe it, why do you think they published this article?

4 FCE

2 Listening

Listen to the beginning of the story. A man will tell you about a strange scientific experiment: he wanted to mesmerize (*hypnotize*, see p. 39) a dying man. For questions 1-6, choose the correct answer — A, B, or C.

1 The narrator first thought of mesmerizing a dying man about

- **A** ☐ nine years ago.
- **B** ☐ nine months ago.
- **C** ☐ three months ago.

2 M. Valdemar had

- **A** ☐ not studied very much.
- **B** ☐ studied a lot.
- **C** ☐ not studied at all.

3 When M. Valdemar talked about dying he was very

- **A** ☐ sad.
- **B** ☐ peaceful.
- **C** ☐ frightened.

4 The narrator knew that

- **A** ☐ M. Valdemar had no relatives.
- **B** ☐ M. Valdemar was married.
- **C** ☐ his relatives would object to his experiment.

5 With regard to the experiment, M. Valdemar appeared to

- **A** ☐ have no particular feelings.
- **B** ☐ be really interested.
- **C** ☐ be fairly interested.

6 When the narrator finally entered M. Valdemar's room for the experiment, he was very surprised because

- **A** ☐ M. Valdemar looked so different.
- **B** ☐ there were so many people with M. Valdemar.
- **C** ☐ M. Valdemar was dead.

We published an article called "The Facts in the Case of M. Valdemar". Numerous people have asked us to print this article again. We are happy to do so. However, there has been much discussion about it—especially with regard to its truth or falsity. You, the reader, can judge for yourself. We know, however, that many people take pride in doubting everything.

The editor of the *Broadway Journal*[1]

It is no surprise that the extraordinary case of M.[2] Valdemar has caused much discussion. It would have been a miracle if it had not. In the beginning, all the people involved did not want the public to know about the story. But a very inaccurate and confused version of the events has appeared, so it is now necessary to give the *facts* of the case. Here they are, as I understand them.

1. **journal** : magazine.
2. **M.** : abbreviation for "Monsieur" (*French for Mr*)

I had studied Mesmerism for about three years. Then, about nine months ago, I realized that, in all the studies on Mesmerism, nobody had ever mesmerized a person *in articulo mortis.* [3] I was particularly curious to see three things. First whether a person who was dying could be mesmerized. Second, whether a dying person's condition made it easier or more difficult to mesmerize him. Third, how much or for how long the arrival of death itself could be stopped.

While I was looking for a subject for these experiments, I thought of my friend, M. Ernest Valdemar, a very educated man. I had already mesmerized him on several occasions, and found I could control him. A few months before I met him, his doctors had told him that he was in the final stages of tuberculosis. He often spoke calmly about his approaching death. He did not see it as a subject to be avoided or regretted.

Also, I knew what his general ideas about scientific research were, and that he would have no objections. I also knew that he had no relatives in America who would object to my experiment. So, I asked him if he wanted to participate, and he said yes. In fact, he seemed quite excited about it. Another advantage was that his disease allowed us to know exactly the period when he would die.

Then, a little more than seven months ago, I received this note from M. Valdemar himself:

My Dear P—,

You can come now if you want. Dr D— and Dr F— agree that I will not live beyond tomorrow midnight, and I think that they are right.

Valdemar

3. ***in articulo mortis*** : (*Latin*) about to die.

I received this note a half an hour after it was written, and in fifteen minutes I was in the dying man's room. I was shocked by the change in his appearance. Now he was incredibly thin. His mental power and his physical strength were still fairly good. When I arrived he was lying in bed writing something in his notebook. Doctors D— and F—were with him.

After holding M. Valdemar's hand for a moment, I went into the next room with the doctors. They told me that the changes in the condition of the patient's lungs had been very rapid. Now, the left lung was totally useless, and the right lung functioned only a tiny bit. It was the opinion of both doctors that M. Valdemar would die about midnight the next day (Sunday). It was then seven o'clock on Saturday evening.

The two doctors left, and I spoke with Valdemar about his approaching death and the experiment. He was very anxious for me to do it. I decided, though, to wait until the next evening when a medical student (Mr Theodore L——l) could be present. I wanted to have somebody reliable present in case something bad happened.

Mr L——l came the next evening, and he took careful notes on all that happened. In fact, the rest of this narrative is mostly based on his notes.

It was about five minutes to eight, when I took M. Valdemar's hand. I then said, "Please tell Mr L——l if you are certain that you want me to do this experiment."

"Yes,' he answered very weakly, "I want to be mesmerized. But I am afraid that you have waited too long."

I began the process of mesmerizing him. I began moving my hand back and forth across his forehead. I used all my powers but nothing happened.

The text and **beyond**

1 Comprehension check

Answer the questions below.

1 Why did the narrator decide to write about his experiments with M. Valdemar?
2 What three things did the narrator want to discover in his experiment?
3 Why was M. Valdemar such a good subject for the experiment?
4 Who was Mr L——l?
5 Why was he present during the experiment?
6 How was M. Valdemar physically and mentally when the narrator came to perform the experiment?
7 How did M. Valdemar react to the narrator's attempts to mesmerize him?
8 How long before he wrote the article did the narrator perform his experiment?

"It would have been a miracle if it had not."

This was the real situation: *M. Valdemar was in favor of experiments on mesmerism so I asked him to take part in my experiments.*

If we want to talk about something that did not really happen, we can say: *If M. Valdemar had not been in favor of experiments on mesmerism, I would not have asked him to take part in my experiments.*

This is the Third Conditional and it is formed in this way: *If M. Valdemar had suffered from a different disease, I would have chosen somebody else.*

If + had + PAST PARTICIPLE, would + have + PAST PARTICIPLE.

2 Third conditional

Fill in the gaps with the infinitives in the box. Then turn these sentences into a Third Conditional with a similar meaning.

take   write   make   ask   be   know   not to feel

1 Poe ***wrote*** a story about mesmerism because the public was interested in the subject.
If the public had not been interested in the subject, Poe would not have written a story about mesmerism.

2 The editor reprinted this article because many people ***asked*** him to see it again.
If many people hadn't asked him to see it again, the editor would not have reprinted the article.

3 The first version of the case of M. Valdemar to appear in newspapers .... very confused because the facts did not come directly from the people involved.

4 The narrator .... embarrassed about asking M. Valdemar to participate in his experiment because M. Valdemar saw death as a perfectly natural subject.

5 The narrator was able to mesmerize M. Valdemar when he was about to die because M. Valdemar .... fairly precisely the time of his death.

6 The narrator was able to write a complete description of his experiment because a medical student .... notes.

7 The doctors .... a good estimate of when he would die because they knew the exact condition of his lungs.

FCE 3 Mesmerism

For questions 1-10 read the text about Franz Anton Mesmer, and decide which answer – A, B, C or D – best fits each gap.

The type of hypnosis described (**0**) ..C.. Poe in his story "The Facts in the Case of M. Valdemar" was (**1**) .... by a German scientist named Franz Anton Mesmer (1734-1815). Mesmer believed that diseases and illness (**2**) .... be caused by blocking the electromagnetic forces of the body, (**3**) .... he called "animal magnetism". Mesmer performed his first experiments with magnets, (**4**) .... later he developed a method of hypnotizing people. Mesmer first worked in Vienna (**5**) .... he was forced to leave. He then went to Paris. At first Mesmer was (**6**) .... successful. Once again, though, the local doctors began to protest. In 1785 a royal commission was set (**7**) .... to investigate Mesmer's methods. It included some of the most (**8**) .... scientists of the day – Antoine Lavoisier, the founder of modern chemistry, the American Benjamin Franklin and Dr. Joseph Guillotin. Their report began, "Animal magnetism may exist without being useful, but it cannot be useful if it does not exist." The report then described their scientific experiments that (**9**) .... that "animal magnetism" did not exist. However, the commission did say that some diseases and illnesses were only in the patients' imagination, and that perhaps Mesmer did cure these patients with his trance. Today, doctors recognize the effectiveness of hypnosis in treating (**10**) .... psychological problems

0	A from	B with	C by	D through
1	A created	B prepared	C produced	D developed.
2	A could	B need	C would	D had
3	A what	B how	C who	D which
4	A and	B but	C however	D though
5	A then	B until	C when	D next
6	A much	B very	C real	D lot
7	A up	B down	C on	D to
8	A know	B considered	C thought	D famous
9	A revealed	B told	C showed	D exposed
10	A much	B very	C lots	D many

Before you read

1 Vocabulary

Match the pictures to the words below. Use a dictionary to help you.

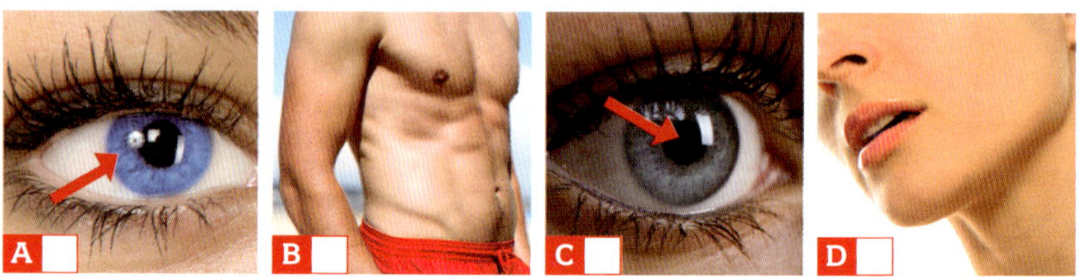

1 pupil **2** jaw **3** chest **4** iris

2 Listening

Listen to the beginning of Part II and answer the questions below.

1 When did the two doctors get there?
2 When did the narrator succeed in mesmerizing M. Valdemar?
3 What did they use to see if M. Valdemar was breathing?
4 What did the narrator ask M. Valdemar?
5 What did M. Valdemar answer?

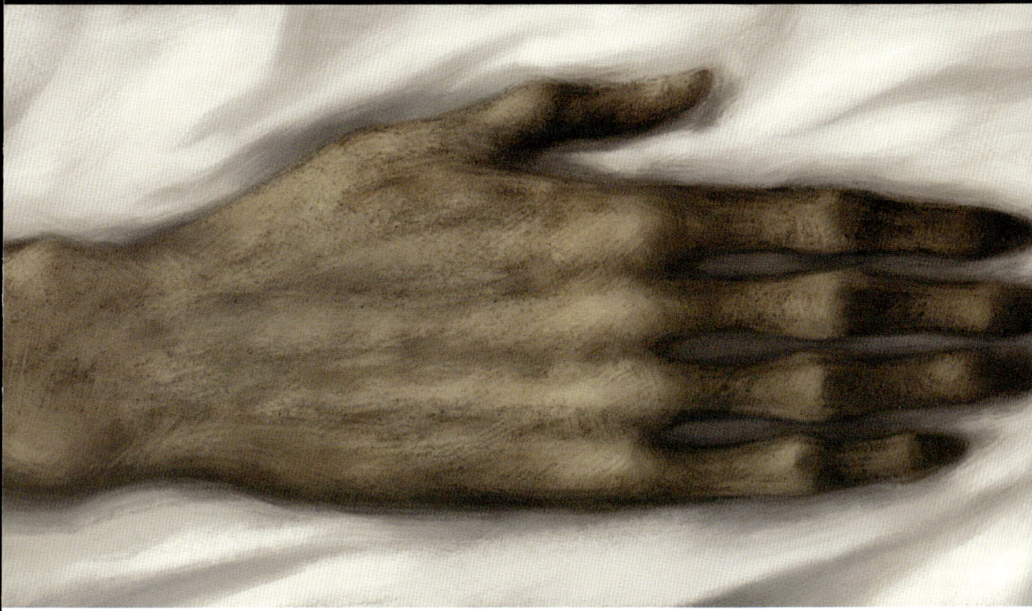

A few minutes after ten, Doctors D— and F— arrived. I explained to them quickly what I was doing, and they had no objections. They told me that the patient was already in the process of dying. I then began to move my hand up and down over the patient's forehead, and to stare into his right eye. 5

Now, his pulse [4] was almost imperceptible, and his breathing loud and difficult. Nothing changed for a quarter of an hour, and then the patient sighed very loudly. His breathing was quiet now.

At five minutes before eleven I could see clear signs that M. Valdemar was mesmerized. He was lying down on the bed, and he appeared to be sleeping. Both doctors said that he was perfectly mesmerized. We then left M. Valdemar alone until three o'clock in the morning.

4. **pulse** : the regular beating of blood caused by the heart.

When we returned, he was still mesmerized. His pulse was imperceptible[5] and we could only tell he was breathing if we put a mirror close to his mouth. His eyes were closed naturally. His arms and legs were rigid and as cold as stone. Still, he did not seem to be dead.

I then tried to make his right arm follow the movements of my right arm. In earlier experiments, I had not succeeded in doing this with M. Valdemar, but now his arm moved with mine. I decided to try and speak with him.

"M. Valdemar," I said, "are you asleep?" He didn't answer, but his lips trembled slightly, so I asked again. His eyelids opened enough to reveal the white of the eye, and then I heard a very, very soft whisper:

"Yes;—asleep now. Do not wake me!—let me die so!"

I now felt his arm and legs. They were still hard and cold. But his right arm followed my hand as before.

"Do you still feel pain in your chest, M. Valdemar?" I asked.

This time he answered immediately, but his voice was even softer than before:

"No pain—I am dying."

We waited until sunrise before we disturbed the patient again.

"M. Valdemar, are you still sleeping?" I said.

After a few minutes he answered, "Yes; still asleep—dying."

The doctors now said that we should leave the patient undisturbed and wait for death to come. We all agreed that he would die in a few minutes. I decided, however, to speak to him once more.

While I was speaking to him, his appearance changed greatly. The eyes opened slowly and the pupils moved upwards and

5. **imperceptible** : so slight or soft that it is difficult to feel or notice.

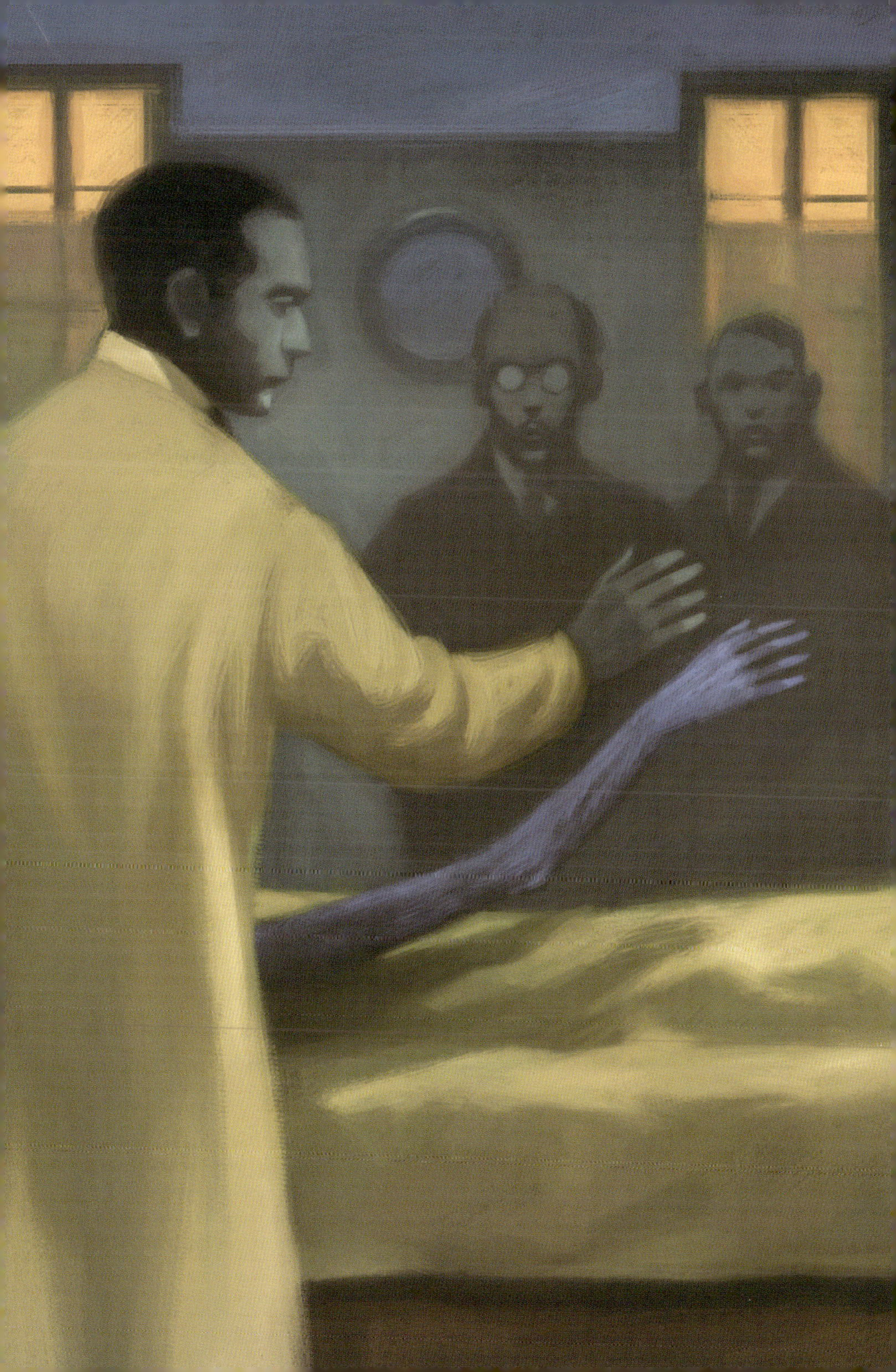

disappeared. His skin became like white paper. Then his upper lip moved back and revealed his teeth, and his lower jaw fell down. Now we could see his tongue, which had become swollen[6] and black. Everybody in the room was used to seeing dead and dying people, but we were all horrified by this sight.

I now feel that every reader will have difficulty believing what follows. Still, I must continue and tell what happened.

"Are you still asleep?" I asked him, but he did not answer. There was no longer any sign of life. We concluded that he was finally dead. We were about to leave the room when we saw that his tongue started vibrating. This continued for a minute, and then a voice came out of his motionless jaws. I cannot describe this voice, this sound – it was broken, it was like nothing on earth.

Still, it was clear that M. Valdemar *spoke*—he was obviously answering the question I had asked a few minutes earlier. He now said:

"Yes;—no;—I *have been* sleeping—and now—now—*I am dead*."

All of us were horrified. Now, even with a mirror in front of his mouth, we could see no sign of breathing. Dr F— tried to take some blood from his arm, but couldn't. I tried to use my mesmeric influence to move his arm. But that did not work now.

It was ten o'clock in the morning. Two nurses arrived to stay with the patient. The two doctors, Mr L—l and I left the house.

In the afternoon, we came back again to see the patient. His condition remained precisely the same. We agreed that we should not awaken him, and that death (or what we usually called death) had been blocked by the Mesmerism. We were certain that if we awakened M. Valdemar, he would instantly die.

From this period until the end of last week—a period of nearly

6. **swollen** : increased in volume.

seven months—we continued to visit M. Valdemar every day. We often went with other doctors. His condition remained the same.

Then last Friday, we finally decided to awaken him.

I used the usual techniques for waking someone who is mesmerized. These did not work at first. Then I saw the first sign of awakening—the iris of his eye rolled down partially. But yellow liquid with a bad smell came out of the eyes at the same time.

The doctors then asked me to see if I could influence his arm again. I tried without success. Then Dr. F— asked me to ask him a question. I did so as follows:

"M. Valdemar, can you explain to us what your feelings are now?"

A red color returned to his cheeks immediately, and his tongue moved violently in his mouth, although his jaws and lips remained rigid. Finally, in the same horrible voice that I described before he said:

"For God's sake!—quick!—quick!—put me to sleep—or, quick!—waken me!—quick!—*I say to you that I am dead!*"

I was totally confused and did not know what to do. At first, I tried to mesmerize him again. But this was not successful, so I tried to awaken him again. Soon I saw that I would be successful—or at least I imagined that my success would be complete—and I am sure that everybody in the room thought that the patient would then awaken.

However, it was impossible for any human being to be prepared for what really happened.

As I quickly performed the necessary procedures to awaken him—while the words "Dead! Dead!" continued to come out of his mouth—within one single minute or even less, his body shrunk—went to pieces and rotted away in my hands. On the bed, before everybody, there was now a mass of rotten liquid.

The text and **beyond**

FCE 1 Comprehension check

For questions 1-5, choose the answer — A, B, C or D — which you think, fits best according to the text.

1 When M. Valdemar was mesmerized, the narrator could tell he was alive from his

A ☐ legs.
B ☐ pulse.
C ☐ arms.
D ☐ breathing.

2 In earlier experiments, M. Valdemar had

A ☐ talked more.
B ☐ appeared to be dead.
C ☐ been less difficult to manipulate.
D ☐ more difficult to manipulate.

3 The narrator thinks that his readers will have a hard time believing that

A ☐ a person who shows every sign of being dead can speak.
B ☐ doctors would accept to perform such a strange experiment.
C ☐ a dying man would really want to be mesmerized.
D ☐ a dying man who is mesmerized can speak.

4 The narrator kept M. Valdemar in a mesmerized state for seven months because

A ☐ he did not know how to awaken him.
B ☐ he thought he would suffer when he awakened him.
C ☐ it was the mesmerism that kept him alive.
D ☐ he thought that mesmerism could cure him.

5 Which one of the following WAS NOT proved by the narrator's experiment?

A ☐ A dying person can be mesmerized.
B ☐ Death can be blocked by Mesmerism.
C ☐ A mesmerized person knows he is dying.
D ☐ Decomposition is blocked by Mesmerism.

FCE 2 The epoch of the hoax

For questions 1-10, read the text below and think of the word which best fits each gap. Use only one word in each gap.

"The Facts in the Case of M. Valdemar" first appeared in a magazine in 1845, but not as a short story — it was published as a true account of a scientific experiment. And it was widely believed. (**0**) ......When....... a newspaper man from Scotland wrote to its author — a not very famous writer named Edgar Allan Poe — and asked him whether it was true or not, Poe responded that the (**1**) .... word to describe this piece of writing was hoax, or trick. Poe later wrote (**2**) .... he lived in the "epoch of the hoax".

(**3**) .... are several reasons why hoaxes became so plentiful in the 1830s and 40s. First printing presses became powered by steam and (**4**) .... print millions of newspapers in a day, for the first time in history. Then, the owners of newspapers soon discovered that nothing sold newspapers better (**5**) .... extravagant and believable — at least for enough time to sell papers — hoaxes.

Before the article on M. Valdemar, in 1835 Poe (**6**) .... already written another hoax article for a New York City newspaper. It was about a man (**7**) .... went to the moon in a hot-air balloon. This hoax was not very successful, partly because another newspaper, *The Sun*, started publishing articles by (or so it said!) the famous astronomer Sir John Herschel. Herschel described a fabulous new telescope with (**8**) .... he made many interesting discoveries, including life on the moon. He said that there were forests, seas, quartz pyramids, unicorns and even a Vespertilio-homo (Latin for "batman"!). *The Sun* never admitted that these stories were a hoax.

Poe had better luck with (**9**) .... hoax, the Great Balloon Hoax of 1844. He wrote a newspaper article saying that Monk Mason (a real hot-air balloon pilot) had crossed the Atlantic Ocean in just three days — truly incredible when a ship took more than a month. Poe wrote in this article that, "The air, as well as the earth and the ocean, has been conquered (**10**) .... science, and will become a common and convenient highway for mankind." This was not just exciting fiction (*or, in other words, an entertaining lie*). It was also great science fiction.

INTERNET PROJECT

Wells & Welles

Another famous American science fiction hoax was carried out by Orson Welles. To find out more about this hoax connect to the Internet and go to www.blackcat-cideb.com. Insert the title or part of the title of the book into our search engine. Open the page for *American Horror*. Click on the Internet project links.
With your partner write a short report about this hoax. You can even let your class hear part of the original radio broadcast.

Say:

- when and where the hoax took place
- how it was done
- what famous science fiction novel was used
- who the author of this novel was
- who Orson Welles was
- whether people believed the hoax

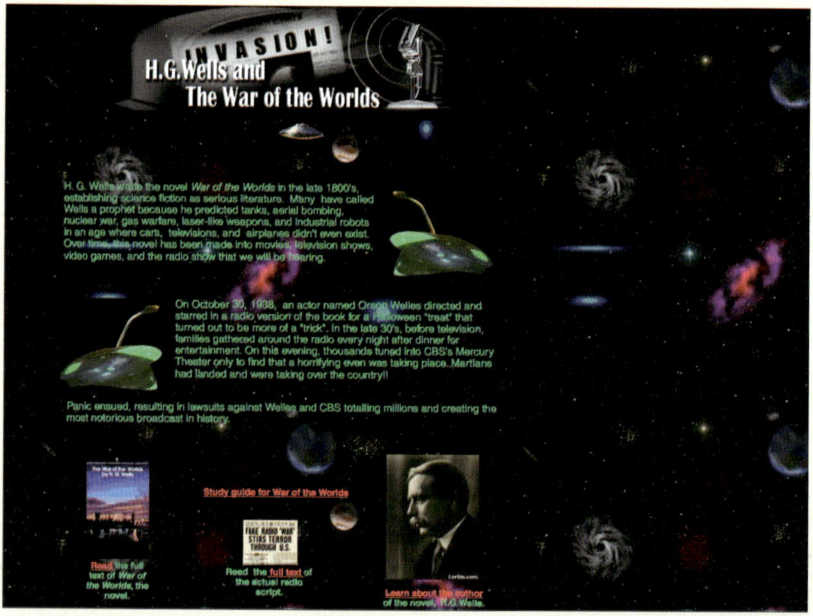

The Black Cat

Before you read

1 Spirit of perverseness

In this and other stories Poe talks about a "spirit of the perverse". He says that it is a basic part of human nature, and defines it as the desire to do things only because we know that we shouldn't do them: a desire to do something that will hurt ourselves – a self-destructive spirit. Discuss this concept with your partner. Can you think of any examples of the "Spirit of the Perverse" from your own lives?

- you could have easily studied for a test but you didn't
- you know wearing a helmet is the best thing to do when you're on the scooter, but you don't
- you tell a friend something that you know will hurt her feelings

2 Vocabulary

Match the pictures to the words below. Use a dictionary to help you.

1 noose   2 pocketknife   3 barrel   4 bas-relief

3 Listening

FCE

Listen to the beginning of Part I. You will hear about the narrator's relationship with animals. For questions 1-7, complete the sentences.

1 What has happened to the narrator is strange and ....
2 When he was young, the narrator was very fond of ....
3 Pluto was the narrator's ....
4 It was so intelligent that the narrator's wife said that it was a ....
5 The narrator began to act differently because he ....
6 Pluto bit the narrator because it was ....
7 The day after he hurt Pluto, the narrator felt ....

I do not think people will believe my story. But I am not mad, and I am not dreaming. Tomorrow I will die and I want to make a confession. The events which I am going to describe here have terrified me, have tortured me, have destroyed me. To me they seemed horrible and supernatural, but perhaps somebody who is calmer and more rational will find a logical explanation. This is my story.

I was a very kind and gentle child who loved animals. As I grew up this love for animals became greater. This is easy to understand: it is difficult to trust people, but you can always trust a faithful dog.

I married when I was young and my wife liked animals too. We had birds, goldfish, a dog, rabbits, a small monkey, and a cat. This cat was quite large, beautiful, completely black and extremely intelligent. In fact, my wife sometimes said that our

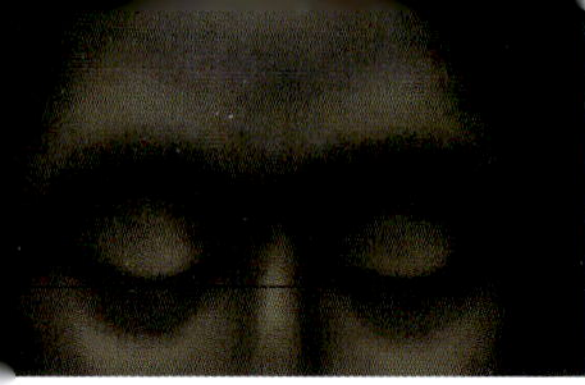

cat was probably a witch in disguise. She was not really serious about this, and I mention it now only because by chance I remember it. Pluto — this was the cat's name — was my favorite pet and playmate. He followed me everywhere.

Unfortunately, I became a victim of alcohol. I drank more and more. Of course, my personality changed. I became moody [1] and irritable with my wife and pets. At the beginning, though, I respected Pluto and never hurt him. But one night I returned home very drunk. I thought that Pluto was avoiding me. I held him violently and in his fright [2] the cat bit my hand. I became furious. I was possessed by a demon. I caught the cat again. Then I took a pocketknife from my pocket, opened it and cut out his eye! I blush, [3] I burn while I now write these facts. The next day I felt horror for my action, but I continued to drink, and wine made me forget the horrible thing I had done.

The cat got better. The empty eye socket [4] was frightening, but the cat was no longer in pain. He went about the house as usual, but, obviously, he ran away from me in terror. At first I was sorry about this, but soon it made me angry. And then came the spirit of PERVERSENESS. Philosophy does not talk about this spirit, but it is a fundamental part of the human heart. We have all done stupid or terrible things simply because we know that we should not do them. This, then, is PERVERSENESS.

1. **moody** : if your mood changes rapidly for no apparent reason, you are moody.
2. **fright** : sudden feeling of fear.
3. **blush** : my face becomes red because I am embarrassed for the bad thing I did.
4. **eye socket** : the hole that contains the eye.

This spirit of perverseness, I say, destroyed me because one day I decided to kill poor Pluto. With tears in my eyes and sadness in my heart I put a noose around his neck and hanged him from a tree. I hanged Pluto only because I knew he loved me, only because he had never hurt me, only because I knew that God would never pardon me for the crime.

The night of this crime there was a fire in my house. My wife, my servant and I just managed to escape. My entire wealth was destroyed in the fire and I lost all hope. I do not want to say that there is a connection between my crime and the fire. I only want to record the facts of my story.

The day after the fire I went to visit the ruins of my house. [5] Only one wall remained, and around this wall was a group of people. They were saying things like "strange!", "singular!". I went closer and saw a strange bas-relief on the wall, the figure of a gigantic cat. The image was extremely accurate. There was a rope about the animal's neck.

When I first saw the image of the cat I was terrified, but I thought about it and found a good explanation. I had hung the cat in the garden next to my house. When the fire began, this garden filled up with people. Somebody probably threw the cat through my bedroom window in order to wake me. The other walls of the house fell in and pressed the body of the cat against this wall. The great heat of the fire and a chemical reaction then made the image.

Although I had a logical explanation, that bas-relief made a great impression on my imagination. For months I could not

5. **ruins of my house** : what remains of the house.

escape the phantasm of the cat. I even tried to find another cat to substitute it. Then, one night in a bar, I saw a black object on top of some barrels of rum. I looked closer. It was a large black cat. It was almost identical to Pluto except it had an indistinct white area on its breast. I caressed the cat and it immediately got up and purred.[6] It was happy. This was the animal I was looking for. I asked the bartender if I could buy it. He said that it was not his. I continued to caress the cat and when I left the bar, the cat followed me home.

My wife liked this cat very much. But I began to dislike it. I had thought that I would be happier with a new cat. Instead, the affection of the cat only disgusted me. And slowly this disgust became hatred. I avoided it because I felt some shame for killing Pluto and I did not want to hurt it too. In addition, this cat, just like Pluto, had only one eye.

6. **purred** : made a long vibrating sound with the throat.

The text and **beyond**

1 Comprehension check

Match the phrases in column A, with the phrases in column B. There are three phrases in column B that you do not need to use.

A

1 ☐ The narrator has always been very fond of animals
2 ☐ The narrator was extremely embarrassed
3 ☐ The narrator killed Pluto
4 ☐ The narrator thought that someone threw Pluto into his room
5 ☐ The neighbors were amazed when they saw the ruins of the house
6 ☐ The narrator wanted the cat he saw in the bar
7 ☐ The narrator did not want to be near the new cat

B

A because he knew he should not do it.
B because he was afraid that he would kill it too.
C because the cat's image was reproduced on a wall.
D because he had hurt Pluto.
E because he wanted to wake him up.
F because he often drank too much.
G because Pluto bit him.
H because they are dependable.
I because it seemed to hate him.
J because he wanted to escape the spirit of Pluto.

2 Instinct versus reason

7 FCE

You will hear Edgar Allan Poe talk about human reason, the instinct of animals, his favorite black cat and a thumb lock for a door. For questions 1-8, complete the sentences. Before listening look at the picture of the thumb lock. Can you understand how it works?

1 People want to feel .... to animals so they say they cannot reason.
2 The habits of .... are superior to the typical thinking of human beings.
3 All .... are witches.

4 This cat has a very .... nature.
5 Poe's cat prefers staying in ....
6 To enter the kitchen, you must push the door, while the thumb-latch is ....
7 The cat can do this with ....
8 When Poe sees his cat opening the kitchen door, he thinks of the difference between ....

3 Speaking

Poe says that the difference between human reason and the instinct of animals is quite small. In fact, once scientists said that only humans could make tools. Now we know that whales, birds and chimpanzees all make and use tools. Now, scientists are even discovering many interesting things in common between human language and the vocal and body language of chimpanzees and the vocal language of whales. What do you think? Discuss the following questions with your partner and then present your ideas to the class.

- Is human reason really superior to animals?
- Do you think many people believe that animals can think?
- Do animals have feelings just like us? Fear? Anger? Jealousy? Love? Loyalty?
- Have you ever seen an animal do something that made you think that it could reason?

T: GRADE 7

4 Speaking: national customs

Edgar Allan Poe had a very high opinion of animals, especially dogs and cats. He obviously enjoyed having them around for their company. In this he is like many Americans today: millions of Americans have either a dog or a cat, and many consider them as members of the family. But this is not the situation all over the world. Present a short report to the class about how dogs and cats and other pets are considered in your country. Say:

1 whether dogs are used mostly for companionship, hunting, police work or guarding property
2 whether it is common to have pets
3 what animals are kept as pets

4 why they are kept as pets. Beauty? Company?
5 whether dogs and cats are considered as members of the family
6 what your opinion of pets is

Before you read

1 Vocabulary

Match the pictures to the words below. Use a dictionary to help you.

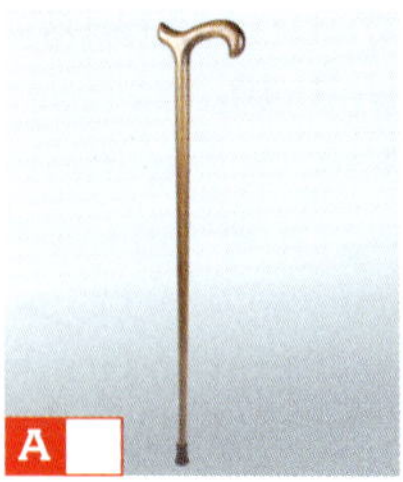

1 axe **2** gallows **3** crowbar **4** cane

2 Prediction

How do you think the narrator will behave with the new cat ?

3 Listening

Listen to the beginning of Part II. You will hear about the tragedy caused by the new cat. Read the following statements and say whether they are true (T) or false (F).

		T	F
1	The cat avoided the narrator.	☐	☐
2	When the narrator wanted to kill the cat, he stopped because he remembered his crime against Pluto.	☐	☐
3	The white area on the cat seemed to change.	☐	☐
4	He dreamed that the cat was on his face.	☐	☐
5	He began to hate everybody.	☐	☐
6	When the narrator almost fell, he killed the cat.	☐	☐

However, the more I hated this cat, the more it followed me. It is difficult to explain how terrible this was. When I sat down it often jumped on my legs and covered me with horrible caresses. When I got up to walk it was between my legs and I almost fell. This made me so angry that I wanted to kill it, but I was stopped — not by the memory of my first crime — but by absolute fear of the beast.

This fear was not exactly a fear of physical evil, but I do not know how to define it. I am almost ashamed to admit — as I wait here in my prison cell — that my terror was caused by something incredibly insubstantial. My wife had often talked about the indistinct white area on the cat's breast, the only difference between him and Pluto. But this indistinct white area gradually became distinct. I tried to ignore what I saw. I said to myself that it was just my imagination. But this distinct image was the real

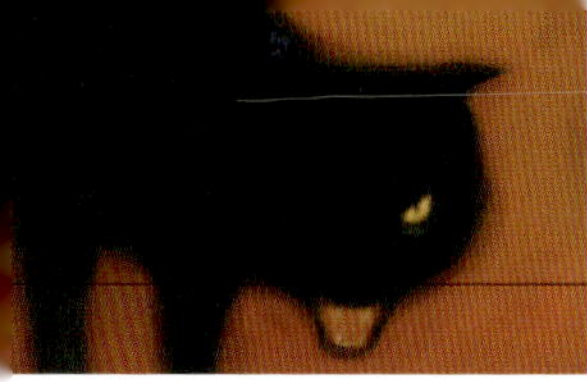

reason why I did not dare hurt the beast. It was an image that I feared. It was the image of the GALLOWS! That terrible instrument of Horror and of Crime — of Agony and of Death!

Oh how I suffered! You cannot imagine. I had killed a brute beast, [7] and now another brute beast was destroying me. Day or night I could not rest. During the day the creature never left me alone, and at night I woke up hourly from terrible dreams with that thing on my face. It was a living nightmare, always there in my heart.

All my good thoughts had gone. Evil thoughts filled my brain. I began to hate all things and all mankind. My wife, I am sorry to say, suffered the most.

One day we had to go down into the cellar. The cat went between my legs. I almost fell. I became furious. I grabbed an axe and tried to kill the animal, but my wife blocked my arm. This made me even more furious and I lifted the axe again and buried it in her brain. She fell dead immediately, without making a sound.

I had murdered her. Now I had to eliminate the body. There were many possibilities. I could cut the body into little pieces and then burn them, or I could bury it.

Finally, I decided to put it inside the wall of the cellar. There was a projection in the wall. I pulled out the bricks with a crowbar. I put the body in there and then I carefully put back the bricks. Nobody could see the difference. It was perfect.

Then I went to look for the cat to kill it too. But the beast had escaped. I did not see it that night. I was finally free of its torment and that night I slept tranquilly, even though I had just killed my wife.

7. **brute beast** : unthinking animal.

The second and the third day passed. The monster did not return. My happiness was supreme. The police came and searched the house, but, of course, they found nothing. I would be happy forever!

Then on the fourth day the police came again. They told me to come with them while they searched the house. They went down into the cellar again and found nothing. I was so happy that I wanted to say something. I wanted to show that I was really not guilty.

"Gentlemen," I finally said, "I am glad that you have no more suspicions. Oh, by the bye, [8] isn't this a well-constructed house. (Now I can't really remember what I said.) In fact, I think it's an excellently well-constructed house. These walls — are you going, gentlemen? — are really solid."

Then in that moment I hit the walls with my cane.

May God protect me! The noise of my cane was answered by a voice from the tomb! At first, the voice was difficult to hear. It was like a child crying. Then it became louder and louder. One long, loud, and continuous scream, completely inhuman that came directly from hell!

For a moment the police and I did not move. But then they easily opened the wall. There inside was the standing corpse, already greatly decayed [9] and covered with blood. On the corpse's [10] head, with its red mouth open and one eye, was the beast, the beast that had made me murder my wife. And now that monster had given me to the hangman. I had shut the monster inside the tomb of my wife!

8. **by the bye** : by the way.
9. **decayed** : decomposed, rotten.
10. **corpse's** : dead body's.

The text and **beyond**

1 Comprehension check

Answer the following questions.

1 Why was the narrator's fear "insubstantial"?
2 How did the cat torment the narrator?
3 Why did the narrator murder his wife?
4 What did the narrator think about after he killed his wife?
5 How did he hide the corpse?
6 After he had hid the corpse, what did he want to do?
7 Why did the narrator think his happiness was perfect?
8 After the police had searched his house and found nothing, why did the narrator start talking again?
9 Why did the cat start screaming?
10 Where had the cat been?
11 How did the Spirit of Perverseness act in this part of the story?

2 Speaking: a mad, logical and supernatural story

Perhaps Poe's horror stories still frighten because it is clear that the terrifying supernatural phenomena are in the narrators' minds. In this story, we are fairly certain that the narrator is mentally ill in some way. But we also believe much of what he says. (Some people, think all of what Poe's narrators say is a product of their imagination!) Report your ideas to the class.

Here are some elements of the story. With your partner discuss whether they

- are real or logical or, at least, possible;
- are products of the narrator's imagination or his madness;
- are supernatural phenomena (if the narrator is not mad).

1 The black cat was a witch in disguise.

2 The narrator cut out Pluto's eye.

3 His house burned down after he hurt Pluto.

4 The gigantic bas-relief on the wall.

5 He really saw another cat.

6 The other cat was not Pluto but a cat that looked like Pluto.

7 The white area began to resemble the gallows.

8 He walled in the cat with the body of his wife.

9 The cat screamed from behind the wall.

"I slept tranquilly, even though I had just killed my wife."

Look at these sentences:
I had just killed my wife, but I slept tranquilly.
= *I slept tranquilly, even though I had just killed my wife.*

Poe became a successful magazine editor, but he never became rich
= *Even though Poe became a successful magazine editor, he never became rich.*

"Although" and "even though" have the same meaning, but "even though" is a bit more emphatic.

3 Clauses with *even though* and *but*

Combine the sentences in the box with the sentences below using *even though* and *but*.

- The narrator could think of a natural explanation for the bas-relief.
- Many parts of the story seem supernatural.
- He is certain people will not believe his story.
- The new cat was very friendly.
- He tried to ignore it.
- The narrator loved animals.
- Poe loved logic and science.
- The narrator hid his wife's corpse very well.

1 He wrote several stories with mad people as narrators.
Even though Poe loved logic and science, he wrote several stories with mad people as narrators.
Poe loved logic and science, but he wrote several stories with mad people as narrators.

2 He is certain that he is not mad.
Even though he thinks people will not believe his story, he is certain that he is not mad.
He is certain that he is not mad, but he thinks people will not believe his story.

3 He thinks a normal person can find a logical explanation.
....
....
....

4 He hurt Pluto.
....
....
....

5 It still frightened him.
....
....
....

6 It disgusted the narrator.
....
....
....

7 He saw that the white area now looked like the gallows.
....
....
....

8 The police found it easily in the end.
....
....
....

4 Vocabulary

Complete the crossword.

Across

2 small mammals, famous for their large ears and for eating carrots

6 very angry

7 masculine possessive adjective

8 animals kept by people for the pleasure of their company

9 the room under ground under a house

12 forgive

13 horror

15 kind

Down

1 the wooden structure to which is attached the rope and noose

3 turn red in the face because you are embarrassed

4 drops of water that come from your eyes when you cry.

5 Killed

10 the opposite of "softer"

11 what remains of a house after some disaster such as a fire

12 the cat made a happy sound = the cat ...

14 opposite of "in"

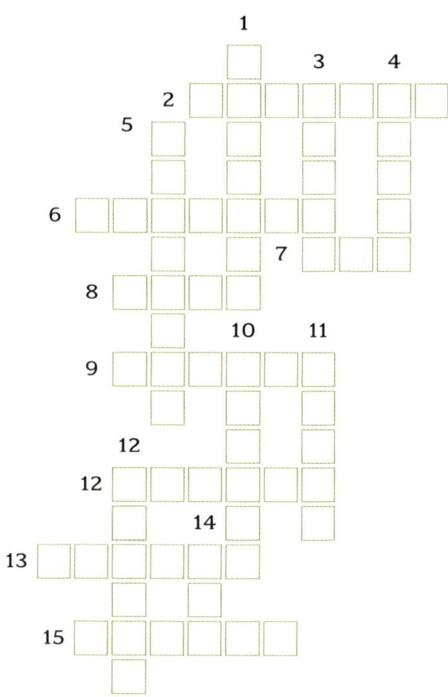

Edgar Allan Poe among many other cultural icons on the cover of the Beatles's famous 1967 album *Sgt Pepper's Lonely Hearts Club Band* (top row).

Poe as pop icon

Just before Halloween 1990, the famous animated sitcom The Simpsons presented a special cartoon version of Edgar Allan Poe's poem, "The Raven". This is not surprising. Edgar Allan Poe is an American cultural icon, just like Elvis Presley, Marilyn Monroe, John F. Kennedy and Coca Cola.

He is especially appreciated by rock bands of all kinds, especially heavy metal. One of Poe's greatest moments in the world of rock 'n' roll was when he appeared on the cover of the famous 1967 album *Sgt. Pepper's Lonely Hearts Club Band* (1967) by the Beatles.

Edgar Allan Poe and his works have also inspired numerous novels and comics. But his greatest influence is in the world of cinema. The

Vincent (1982), directed by Tim Burton.

first film based on his writings appeared in 1910, and films about him or based on his works have been made to this day.

The most famous and influential films of Poe's works were made by the director Roger Corman. They include *House of Usher*, 1960; *The Pit and the Pendulum*, 1961; *The Premature Burial*, 1962; *Tales of Terror*, 1926; *The Raven*, 1963; and *The Masque of the Red Death*, 1964. Most of these films were only half serious and they were similar to the original Poe stories. Roger Corman's favorite actor was Vincent Price.

Almost twenty years later, the film director Tim Burton used Price's voice to narrate a stop-motion film called *Vincent*. This short film was in honor of Vincent Price himself. It was about a young boy named Vincent Malloy who is obsessed with Edgar Allan Poe and Vincent Price. Tim Burton, who directed such famous films as *The Nightmare Before Christmas*, *Batman Returns* and *Charlie and the Chocolate Factory*, says that Roger Corman's Poe was an essential part of his childhood. Certainly, Poe would have appreciated Burton's intelligent mixture of humor, melancholy and horror.

But why has Poe's work become so important in popular culture?

The poster for Roger Corman's 1964 Poe-inspired film starring Vincent Price.

The main reason is that Poe himself wrote his work to appeal to a wide audience. He greatly admired Charles Dickens (1812-1870), who managed to attract a large audience while maintaining his artistic integrity. This became Poe's objective. His stories and poems first appeared in magazines, and Poe wrote stories in the popular fictional genres of the time. His frightening tales like "The Black Cat" and "The Tell-Tale Heart" were like stories you could find in the cheap collection of horror stories called "Penny Dreadfuls" or "Penny Bloods" – the equivalent of today's comic books. Poe also tried to write about the popular topics of his time, like travel in hot-air balloons, cholera epidemics, premature burials and arctic travel. So, his stories and poems entertain on a superficial level, but they are also exquisitely made works of literary art.

Besides his writing, Edgar Allan Poe himself has become a cultural icon. He is seen as the great tormented genius who died young and misunderstood. He is often compared to the first Romantic poets John Keats, Percy Shelley and Lord Byron, who all died young. The legend of the tormented artistic genius became popular again in the

1960s and 70s; various rock musicians were compared to Poe and the other Romantics. Interestingly, the myth of Poe as the tormented and mad genius began immediately after his death as a lie. A man named Rufus Griswold wrote an obituary about Poe. Griswold disliked Poe and lied about him. He said that he was a drunken madman who walked the streets at night. Poe, he wrote, lived in the same nightmare world as his horrible characters.

Serious books now tell the true story of an important literary critic, magazine editor, inventor of various literary genres and fine poet. But the fictional mad and melancholy Edgar Allan Poe is still the most popular of all.

1 Comprehension check

Say whether the following statements are true (T) or false (F), and then correct the false ones.

		T	F
1	Poe's works have appeared in popular American television shows.	☐	☐
2	Some heavy metal rock bands admire Poe's writings.	☐	☐
3	Films based on Poe's stories first appeared in the 1950s.	☐	☐
4	Tim Burton has made many films based on Poe's short stories.	☐	☐
5	Poe's stories of horror sometimes contain humor.	☐	☐
6	Poe wanted his stories to be popular with ordinary readers.	☐	☐
7	Poe was not interested in writing great works of literary art.	☐	☐
8	Poe was a mad, tormented genius.	☐	☐
9	Poe's stories were first published in magazines.	☐	☐
10	"Penny Bloods" were inexpensive collection of horror stories.	☐	☐

The Oval Portrait

Before you read

1 Vocabulary

Match the pictures to the words below. Use a dictionary to help you.

A

B

C

D

E

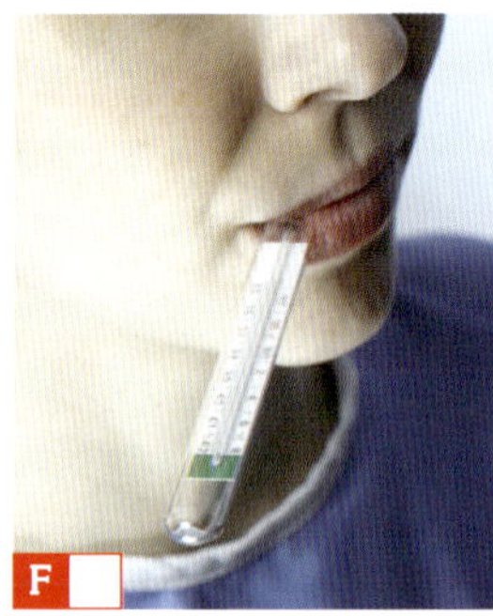
F

G

H

I

1 fever	4 arms	7 palette
2 turret	5 candelabrum	8 easel
3 tapestry	6 brushstroke	9 niche

9 FCE

2 Listening

Listen to the story. You will hear about a man traveling in the Apennine Mountains of Italy with his valet (servant). For questions 1-5, choose the best answer — A, B or C.

1 The narrator was crossing

A ☐ some plains.
B ☐ a wide river.
C ☐ some mountains.

2 The narrator felt bad because he was

A ☐ lonely.
B ☐ afraid.
C ☐ seriously injured.

3 He saw a castle that

A ☐ people had left a short time earlier.
B ☐ was guarded by a few soldiers.
C ☐ was full of many people.

4 Mrs Radcliffe was

A ☐ the owner of the old castle.
B ☐ a woman who wrote about old castles.
C ☐ a woman who liked reading about old castles.

5 The paintings in the room

A ☐ interested the narrator very much.
B ☐ confused the narrator.
C ☐ frightened him a little bit.

My valet Pedro and I were traveling through the Apennine Mountains in Italy. I was badly hurt and had a high fever. We finally saw a very strange and gloomy castle that had been recently abandoned. It was the kind of castle that you can read about in certain old novels about ghosts by Mrs Radcliffe. Pedro knew that I couldn't remain outside in my condition, so he decided to break into the castle. 9

When he had broken in, he took me to a small room in a turret of the castle. This room had many very old paintings, tapestries and arms. There were also many spirited [1] modern paintings. I looked closely at them all. They fascinated me greatly, perhaps because I was delirious from the fever. I also found a book that told the story of each of the paintings in the room.

Pedro lit the candles of a large candelabrum and I began to contemplate each piece of art in this bizarre room. I lay in my bed reading and looking at the paintings for a long, long time. END Then, since Pedro was asleep, I moved the candelabrum so I could read more easily.

1. **spirited** : full of animation.

The light of the candles made it easier to read, but it also illuminated a strange little painting in a dark niche. It was the portrait of a lovely adolescent girl. I do not know why, but I closed my eyes for a moment and thought about it.

Then I opened my eyes to look at it again. Then I wondered why I was so charmed by this painting. Its frame was oval and gold. The painting itself was done very well. It showed the head and shoulders of the girl. The girl herself was extremely beautiful.

The painting had even startled me because for a moment it looked like a living person. Still none of these three things could explain the secret of its mysterious effect on me. Then I discovered the reason: the expression on her face was almost perfectly lifelike. And this lifelikeness had confused me, startled me and filled me with horror.

I immediately looked in the book for the story of this oval portrait, and read the following story:

The girl in the portrait was extremely beautiful and extremely joyous. But it was an evil hour when she married the painter. He was passionate, austere and studious; and he already had a "wife": his Art.

The girl in the portrait was extremely happy, and she loved all things; she only hated the Art which was her rival. She was only afraid of the palette, easel and brushes that took her husband away.

It was therefore a terrible thing for her when her husband asked her to pose for a painting. But she was very humble [2] and obedient, and she agreed to pose.

She posed for this portrait in a cold, unhealthy room of a turret of the castle. The only light in the room came from a small window in the ceiling.

2. **humble** : modest in behaviour, attitude or spirit.

The artist worked with energy and only thought of his work. He became obsessed with capturing every shade and color of life on his young wife's face.

Since the room where she was sitting was cold and damp, she got more and more ill. Still, her husband did not notice. All he noticed was his painting. He was a wild and moody man, and he was often lost in his own private dream world. Everybody else saw that his wife was getting weaker and weaker. Still, she continued smiling and never complained because she saw that he took such great interest in this painting: he worked day and night to paint the woman who loved him and who was becoming more and more ill for this love.

Some of the people who saw him working said, "This painting is truly marvelous. It is proof of both his power as a painter and of his love for his wife."

When the painter was finishing the portrait, nobody was allowed in the turret because the painter had become so passionate about his work: he rarely took his eyes off the canvas to look at his wife's face.

In fact, he had become so obsessed with his work that he did not notice that as he put red and pink on the canvas, red and pink left his young wife's cheeks.

Finally he only needed to add a little bit of color for the mouth and a little bit of color for the eyes. The living color of his wife's face shone again for a moment and then went out like a lamp.

The painter added the last brushstroke and for one moment was entranced in front of his painting. He then became pale and began to tremble. He then cried loudly, "This is indeed Life itself!" Then he looked suddenly at his wife: — She was dead!

The text and **beyond**

1 Comprehension check

Decide whether the following statements are true (T) or false (F), and then correct the false ones.

		T	F
1	The narrator went into the castle to see the paintings.	☐	☐
2	The narrator perceptions and thinking were affected by his illness.	☐	☐
3	The narrator found a book on the history of art in Italy.	☐	☐
4	The narrator became attracted by one painting in particular.	☐	☐
5	The painting of the girl startled him because the girl was so beautiful.	☐	☐
6	The painter was already secretly married when he married the girl.	☐	☐
7	The girl enjoyed life and living.	☐	☐
8	At first, the girl tried not to pose.	☐	☐
9	The painter wanted the painting of his wife to be like a wild dream.	☐	☐
10	The girl never mentioned to her husband that her health was getting worse.	☐	☐
11	The painter was the only one who appreciated his painting.	☐	☐
12	The girl died shortly before the painting was finished.	☐	☐

2 A different point of view

Write a short version of the "The Oval Portrait" in 120-180 words from the girl's point of view.
Include the following information:

- how she felt when she married the painter
- why she agreed to pose
- how she felt when she saw the room where she would pose
- why she never complained.

You can begin the story like this:

The day of my marriage to this great man was ...
... Now I can write no more. I feel my life is leaving me.

FCE 3 Speaking: paintings

Look at these two photographs. They show people experiencing art in different ways. Describe the two photographs to your partner, and say which you would prefer and why.

Look at these two paintings. They represent two different ways of seeing reality. Describe the two paintings to your partner, and say which stimulates your imagination more.

FCE 4 Obsessions

You are going read an adaptation of a short story by Nathaniel Hawthorne (1804-1864) which is often compared to Poe's "The Oval Portrait". Seven sentences have been removed from the story. Choose from the sentences A-H the one which fits each gap (1-7). There is one extra sentence which you do not need to use.

Nathaniel Hawthorne.

The Birthmark [1]

During the late 1700s the discovery of electricity and similar mysteries appeared to many as miracles. However, a scientist named Aylmer left his love of science to marry a woman named Georgiana.
(1) __________ . Sadly, though, one day Aylmer noticed that Georgiana had a small hand-shaped birthmark on her cheek. "If I can remove the birthmark," he said, "the world will have an example of perfect beauty." Aylmer became increasingly disturbed and disgusted by it. (2) __________ "My dear husband," she said, "please

1 **Birthmark** : an unusually coloured mark on the skin that can be seen when someone is born, and lasts for the rest of their life.

remove it, even if I must risk my life!" "Don't worry," he continued, "I am certain that I can do it. And when I have removed it, it will be as if I had created perfect beauty, as if I had created life!"

So, they both went to live in his laboratory. (3) [ ]. When he heard the plan, Aminadab said, "If she were my wife, I would never eliminate that birthmark."

(4) [ ] "Because," he answered, "I have discovered that your birthmark is not superficial. It is connected with the heart of your being and existence. (5) [ ]." "I don't care," said Georgiana. "The only thing that matters is to eliminate that horrible birthmark!"

Aylmer then left her and returned with a glass holding a clear liquid. (6) [ ] Aylmer watched her face as she slept. Slowly the horrible birthmark began to disappear. Finally, she awoke and saw that Aylmer was worried. "(7) [ ] You tried to obtain the best in heaven, and so rejected the best on this earth. Aylmer, dearest Aylmer, I am dying."

A There she met Aminadab, Aylmer's assistant.

B I do not think I will ever be able to eliminate it because it would be too dangerous.

C Do not be sad, my poor Aylmer!

D One day Georgiana saw that her husband was worried and she asked him why.

E She drank it and then fell asleep.

F I have now one medicine for you to try, but it is dangerous!

G Georgiana herself wished to eliminate it.

H She was very beautiful.

5 Speaking – Compare and contrast

With your partner, discuss what Hawthorne's story "The Birthmark" and Poe's story "The Oval Portrait" have in common, and how they are different. Find a couple of examples of each, and present your ideas to the class.

INTERNET PROJECT

Gothic: from Mrs Radcliffe's castles to Ms Rice's vampires.

To find out more about the horrifying and entertaining world of Gothic literature, connect to the Internet and go to www.blackcat-cideb.com. Insert the title or part of the title of the book into our search engine. Open the page for *American Horror*. Click on the Internet project links.

With your partner find out some more interesting facts about a particular area or two of Gothic literature such as:

- the Shelleys
- detective Gothic
- Gothic heroes
- Gothic buildings
- vampires
- the Brontë sisters
- Gothic heroines
- the beginning of Gothic
- Ms Rice's vampires
- or anything else that intrigues you

Women and the Gothic

Women and the Gothic

The Gothic marketplace would seem to be one in which women would hold equal sway. Many Gothic authors were women; even a printer of Gothic romances, Ann Lemoine, was a woman. Author Charlotte Smith, whose life of domestic violence resembled a Gothic novel, was singled out for unique public humiliation by her publisher. Ann Ward Radcliffe preferred to be thought dead or insane than an authoress. And within the world of the Gothic novel, women are subject to numerous assaults on their virtue and to the tyranny of fathers, would-be lovers, and husbands.

Legends of Terror! And Tales of the Wonderful and the Wild. London: G. Creed, 1840. The Sadleir-Black Collection of Gothic Novels. A new series of legends, featuring more disquieting illustrations. Illustrations in the Gothic novel usually featured a beleagured lovely peering anxiously over her shoulder, or a young man terrified by a specter. These are slightly unusual in their explicit focus on death and monsters. The Sadleir-Black Collection of Gothic Novels. PZ2L446 new ser 1840

Legends of Terror! And Tales of the Wonderful and the Wild, Being a Complete Collection of Interesting Legendary Tales, National Romances, and Traditional Relics, in Prose and Verse, Comprising, in Addition to Numerous Original Translations, the Whole of the Ancient Legends of Germany, Scotland, Ireland, Wales, and other Countries, with Historical Illustrations. Embellished with Forty Elegant Engravings in Wood. London: Sherwood, Gilbert, and Piper, 1826. The Sadleir-Black Collection of Gothic Novels. Frederick Coykendall writes, "The book is gruesome and in its illustrations even disgusting" (GB). With this promising beginning, one can peruse this collection of tales from various countries. Usually featuring skeletons and monsters in alternating poses, the illustrations do indeed leave the reader strangely disquieted.

The Tell-Tale Heart

Before you read

1 Speaking : impressions

You are going to a read about a man who begins to hate another man's physical defect. In fact, he will begin to think this physical defect is evil. Obviously, this man is mad. But what about you? With your partner discuss how important the following things are to you when you meet a new person. Then, present some of your ideas to the class.

- physical defects
- accent
- age
- problems in speaking
- taste in clothing
- nationality

2 Vocabulary

Match the pictures to the words below. Use a dictionary to help you.

A

B

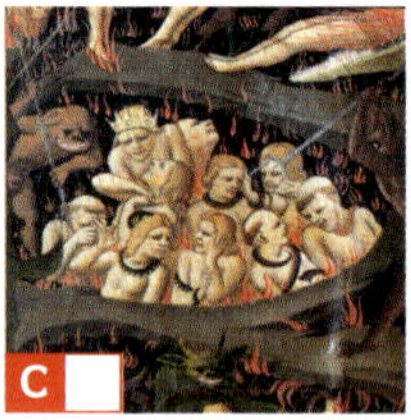
C

D

1 vulture   2 heaven   3 thread of a spider   4 hell

10 3 Listening

Listen to the beginning of Part I. You will hear about a man obsessed with an eye. Then say whether the following statements are true (T) or false (F).

		T	F
1	The narrator says his hearing has improved greatly.		
2	The narrator wants to convince us that he is not mad.		
3	One of the old man's eyes resembled the eye of a vulture.		
4	The narrator decided to kill the old man because of his eye.		
5	The narrator began to treat the old man badly a few days before he killed him.		
6	The narrator looked into the old man's room just after it became dark.		
7	The narrator looked into the old man's room for two weeks.		

TRUE! — nervous — very, very terribly nervous I was and I am. But why will you say that I am mad? The disease made my senses extremely acute. It did not destroy them. My sense of hearing was very good. I heard all things in heaven and on earth. I also heard things in hell. Why, then, am I mad? Listen how healthily I can tell my story.

I cannot say how I first got the idea; but once I had it, this idea never left my brain day or night. There was no reason for this idea. There was no passion. I loved the old man. He had never done anything wrong to me. I did not want his gold. I think it was his eye! Yes, it was this! One of them looked like a vulture's eye — a pale blue eye, with a film [1] over it. When this

1. **film** : thin covering or layer (because the eye is not well).

eye looked at me, my blood became cold. And so, gradually — very gradually — I decided to kill the old man, and eliminate that eye forever.

Well, now you think I am mad. But madmen don't know anything. You would have loved to see me. I did everything so carefully, so intelligently. I was never kinder to the old man than during the whole week before I killed him. And every night, about midnight, I opened his door slowly, very, very slowly. I opened just enough for my head. Then I put in a lantern all closed, closed so that no light came out, and then I put in my head. It was really fantastic how I did this. You would have laughed to see how slowly and intelligently I put my head in his room so that I would not wake him. It took me a whole hour to put my head into his room. Could a madman be so careful? When my head was in his room, I opened the lantern and its light fell on his vulture eye.

I did this same thing for seven nights, but each night his eye was closed, so I could not do my work. The old man did not bother me. His Evil Eye bothered me.

Every morning I walked happily into his room. I asked him if he had slept well. I talked to him like a friend. So you can see that he had to be a very wise man to suspect that every night, just at twelve, I looked at him while he slept.

The eighth night I was more careful than usual when I opened the door. A watch's minute hand moves more quickly than my hand moved. That night I was stronger and more intelligent than I had ever been. I laughed quietly and perhaps the old man heard me because he moved.

You probably think that I pulled my head back — but no. His room was completely dark and I knew that he could not see me. I kept pushing my head in.

I had my head in and was about to open the lantern when the old man jumped up and shouted, "Who's there?"

I did not move and said nothing. For a whole hour I did not move a muscle and I did not hear him lie down again. He was listening.

Then I heard him groan, [2] and I knew it was the groan of mortal terror. It was not a groan of sadness or pain — oh no! — it comes from a horrible feeling at the bottom of your soul. I knew that feeling well. I had that same feeling every night around midnight when I looked at the old man sleeping. I felt sorry for him, but I had to laugh too.

His fear was growing bigger. He tried to convince himself that the noise came from his imagination. He said to himself, "It is just the wind — it is only a mouse running across the floor." Yes, he tried to comfort himself, but he found it all in vain. All in vain, because Death's shadow already covered the old man. And it was Death's invisible shadow that made him feel the presence of my head in the room.

After I had waited for a long time, I decided to open the lantern a little tiny bit. So, I opened it — you cannot imagine how carefully — until a single ray of light, like the thread of a spider, shot out from the lantern and onto the vulture eye.

2. **groan** : a sound expressing sadness or pain – "Ooooooh"

His eye was open — wide, wide open — and I became furious as I looked at it. I saw it perfectly, all pale blue and with the disgusting film over it that made my bones cold; but I could see nothing else of the old man's face or body. I had, by instinct, directed the light right on that horrible spot.

Now I could hear a low sound like the sound of a watch enveloped in cotton. I told you before I was not mad, but my senses were very acute. I knew that sound well, too. It was the beating of the old man's heart. It made me more furious just like the beating of a drum that stimulates a soldier's courage.

The text and **beyond**

FCE 1 Comprehension check

For questions 1-7 choose the answer — A, B, C or D — which you think fits best according to the text.

1 After his illness, the narrator says that he
- A ☐ suffered as if he were in hell.
- B ☐ could hear better than before.
- C ☐ did not want money anymore.
- D ☐ felt as if he were in heaven.

2 The narrator thinks that people with mental illnesses
- A ☐ are very exact in their actions.
- B ☐ can reason carefully.
- C ☐ can hear precisely and well.
- D ☐ are ignorant of everything.

3 The narrator wanted to kill the old man because
- A ☐ he didn't want to see his eye anymore.
- B ☐ the old man hated him.
- C ☐ he wanted to prove that he was not mad.
- D ☐ after the disease he understood that the old man was evil.

4 The narrator finally decided to kill the old man after seven nights because earlier
- A ☐ he couldn't see the vulture eye.
- B ☐ he couldn't hear the old man's heart.
- C ☐ he couldn't hear the old man's voice.
- D ☐ he couldn't feel the old man's fear.

5 What does the narrator think that he had in common with the old man?
- A ☐ acute senses
- B ☐ a terrible fear
- C ☐ a great anger
- D ☐ a horrible pain

6 How does the narrator feel about his plans to murder the old man?

A ☐ confused
B ☐ angry with himself
C ☐ proud of his cleverness
D ☐ afraid of the evil in himself

7 The sound of the old man's heart

A ☐ increased the narrator's anger.
B ☐ frightened the narrator.
C ☐ made him feel sorry for the old man.
E ☐ increased the narrator's feeling of disgust.

2 Similes

When you compare two different things using "like" or "as", we call this figure of speech a simile. Poe uses four similes, or comparisons with "like" in this part of the story. Discuss them with your partner and decide what you think he wanted to communicate. Some possible answers are given for the first two. You can add your own. Find your own answers for the last two. Compare your results with the rest of the class.

1 The old man had an eye "like a vulture". Vultures eat dead animals. The narrator thought that

A ☐ the eye will bring death.
B ☐ an animal that eats dead, rotten animals must be evil.

2 The light of the lantern shot out "like the thread of a spider". This communicates

A ☐ the idea of a spider capturing its prey/the narrator killing the old man.
B ☐ the precision of the ray of light.

3 The heart of the old man was "like a watch enveloped in cotton".

4 The heart made him furious "just like the beating of a drum".

FCE 3 Sentence transformation

For questions 1-7, complete the second sentence so that it has a similar meaning to the first sentence, using the word given. Do not change the word given. You must use between two and five words, including the word given. Here is an example (0).

0 My sense of hearing was very good.
COULD
I ....could hear very.................. well.

1 This idea never left my brain day or night.
ABOUT
I .... and night.

2 I kept pushing my head in.
TO
I .... my head in.

3 The disease did not destroy my senses.
BY
My senses .... the disease.

4 I put my head slowly in his room so that I would not wake him.
WANT
I put my head slowly .... to wake him.

5 I did not move a muscle for a whole hour.
WAS
I .... for a whole hour.

6 He tried to convince himself that the noise came from his imagination.
WAS
He tried to convince himself that he .... the noise.

7 I asked him if he had slept well.
YOU
I asked, '... well?'

T: GRADE 7

4 Speaking: education

Edgar Allan Poe's short stories and his poems are popular among middle-school and high-school American students. For an idea on how Poe is presented in American schools take a look at the excellent education Internet site referred to in the Internet project on page 103.

Other favorites in American schools are: *Romeo and Juliet*, *Macbeth*, *Huckleberry Finn*, *Julius Caesar*, *To Kill a Mockingbird*, *The Scarlet Letter*, *Of Mice and Men*, *Hamlet*, *The Catcher in the Rye*, *The Great Gatsby* and *Lord of the Flies*.

Can you match the titles above with the short descriptions of the stories below? Use an encyclopedia or the Internet to help you.

- The tragic love between two teenagers and the tragic hate of families.
- The frightening adventures of some boys on an island.
- A realistic account of a 17-year-old boy's experiences and feelings after being expelled from school.
- The public shame and dignity of a woman who commits adultery
- Friendship between two farm workers — one quite intelligent, the other mentally disabled — during the Great Depression of the 1930s
- Racism and the destruction of innocence as seen through the eyes of young boy.
- The decadent lifestyle of the rich and famous in the 1920s — the Jazz Age.
- Friendship between a white boy and an escaped African-American slave.
- The assassination of a dictator and its deadly consequences.
- The violent rise and fall of a king and his mad queen.

With your partner prepare a short report comparing the literature that you study and the literature studied in American schools. Use the following questions to help you.

1 Do you think the books studied in American English classes seem interesting? Why or why not?

2 Are any of them studied in your school — in the original English language or in translation?

3 Do you think Poe is a good author for high school students? Why or why not?

4 In general, what kind of books should middle-school and high-school students study?

5 Do you think the books studied by American students look more interesting than the ones studied in your school? If so, why?

Before you read

1 Vocabulary

Match the pictures to the words below. Use a dictionary to help you.

A

B

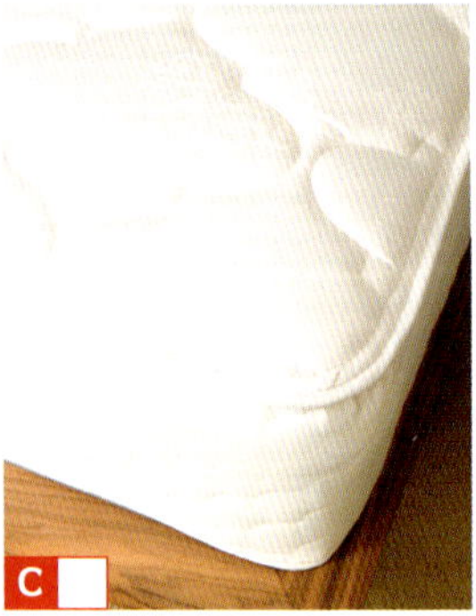
C

1 tub 2 mattress 3 boards

11

2 Listening

FCE

Listen to the beginning of Part II. You will hear why the man finally killed the old man. For questions 1-5, choose the best answer — A, B or C.

1 The sound of the old man's heart became so loud that the narrator thought it

A ☐ would blow up.

B ☐ hurt his ears.

C ☐ wake up the old man.

2 When the narrator finally came into the room, the old man

A ☐ screamed.

B ☐ tried to hit the narrator.

C ☐ pushed the narrator on the floor.

3 To kill the old man, the narrator

A ☐ hit him with lantern.

B ☐ pushed him against the wall.

C ☐ suffocated him with the mattress.

4 To be certain the old man was really dead, the narrator

A ☐ listened for the beating of his heart.

B ☐ put his hand on his chest.

C ☐ watched his eye for many minutes.

5 To hide the body, the narrator put it

A ☐ behind the wall.

B ☐ under the bed.

C ☐ under the floor.

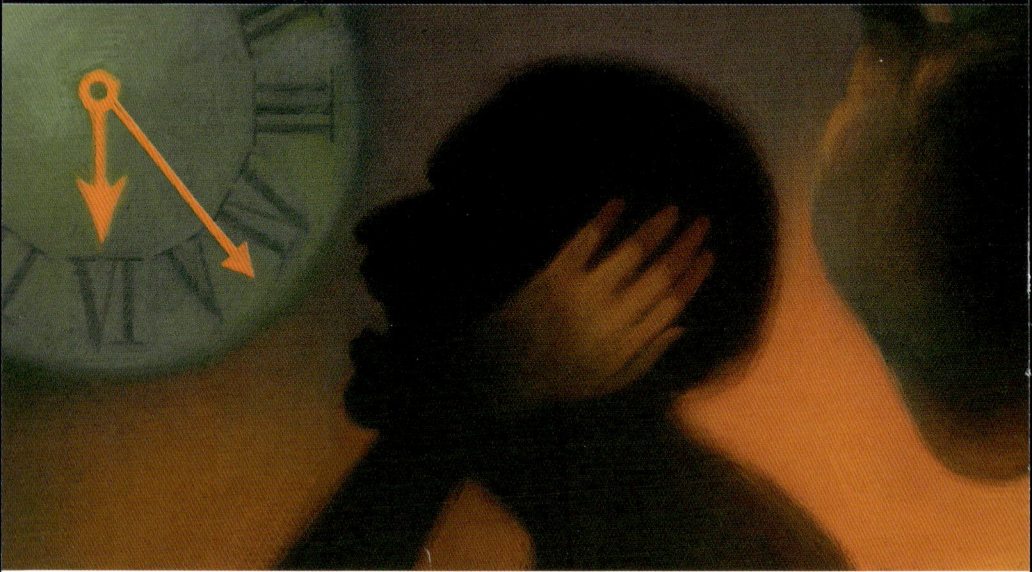

**But I did not move. I hardly breathed. I held the light on the eye. 11
And the beating of the heart increased. It became quicker and quicker, and louder and louder. The old man's terror must have been extreme. It grew louder, I say, louder every moment! — do you understand? I told you I am nervous and I really am. That night that strange noise made me do something terrible.**

The beating grew louder, louder! I thought his heart would explode. Then I thought, "Maybe the neighbors will hear it!" It was the old man's moment. With a shout, I opened up the lantern completely and jumped into the room. He screamed once — only once. In an instant I pulled him to the floor and pulled the heavy bed over him. I then smiled happily because I had done so much.

But, for many minutes, the heart continued to beat under the mattress. This, however, did not bother me: the noise could not be heard through the wall.

Finally, it stopped. The old man was dead. I removed the bed and examined the body. Yes, he was stone, stone dead. I placed my hand on his heart and held it there many minutes. There was no more beating. He was stone dead. His eye would trouble me no more.

If you still think that I am mad, listen how carefully I hid the body. The night was ending and I worked carefully and quietly. First, I cut off the head and the arms and the legs. Then I removed some of the boards from the floor and placed the pieces of his body underneath. Then I put back the boards so carefully that no human eye — not even his — could have noticed anything wrong. There was no blood to clean — none at all — because I had been very careful. A tub had caught all the blood — ha! ha! ha!

When I finished my work it was four o'clock and it was still dark. As the bell of the clock rang four times, someone knocked at the door. I went to open it without any fear or worry. I had nothing to be afraid of.

Three men came in. They introduced themselves. They were policemen.

A neighbor had heard somebody scream and had thought something terrible had happened, so they called the police.

I smiled, — what did I have to fear? I told the policemen to come in. I told them that I had screamed because of a bad dream. The old man, I said, was away in the country. I told them to look around, to look everywhere. I took them to his room. I showed them his gold. Then I brought some chairs into the room and put them down over the spot where the body of the victim lay. I told the policemen to sit down and rest a moment.

The policemen were satisfied. I had convinced them. They sat and I talked happily. But, in a few moments, I felt myself getting pale and I wanted them to go. My head ached and I heard a ringing in my ears. But they continued to talk. The ringing became more distinct: I talked more and more to try to eliminate the feeling. Then I discovered that the noise was not in my ears.

I became very pale and I talked louder and louder. But the sound increased — and what could I do? It was a low sound — very much like a watch enveloped in cotton. I could hardly breathe, but the policemen could not hear the sound. I talked more quickly. I talked more loudly, but the noise increased. I stood up and began to argue about stupid things. I shouted, I moved my arms about. Why didn't those policemen leave? I walked around the room quickly — but the noise still increased. Oh God! What could I do? I screamed, I shouted! I pulled the chair over the place where the noise came from, but the noise was still louder, louder — louder! And still the men talked happily and smiled.

Didn't they hear? Oh God! No, no! They heard! — they suspected! — they knew! — they were making fun of my horror! This I thought and this I think. But anything was better than this agony, than their making fun of me! I could not bear their hypocritical smiles any more. I felt that I must scream or die! — and now again! — Listen! Louder! Louder! Louder! Louder! —

"Villains!" I screamed, "do not pretend any more! I admit what I did! — Pull up the boards! — Here! here! It's the beating of his hideous heart!"

The text and **beyond**

1 Comprehension check

Match the phrases in column A with the phrases in column B. There are three phrases in column B that you do not need to use.

A

A The narrator finally decided to kill the old man
B The old man's eye stopped troubling the narrator
C The body fit under the boards
D A neighbor called the police
E The narrator smiled at the police
F The narrator began talking louder
G The narrator was certain that the policemen smiled
H The narrator told the policemen to pull up the boards

B

1 because he had heard a scream.
2 because the narrator had cut it up into pieces.
3 because he wanted to hide the noise.
4 because he could not stand hearing the beating heart.
5 because they were enjoying his horrible situation.
6 because the old man was dead.
7 because he was certain that he had hidden the body perfectly.
8 because he didn't want the neighbors to hear the beating heart.
9 because they were happy that the old man was dead.
10 because he wanted to show the policemen he was innocent.
11 because he thought the old man would try to escape.

2 Meanings

With your partner, look at the dictionary definitions below, and then decide what you think Poe meant by a "tell-tale heart". There are some possible answers below. You can modify these answers or give your own. Justify your answers. Report your ideas to the class.

Heart *noun*: 1. The muscular organ that pumps blood. 2. The center of a person's emotions and sincerest feelings. 3. Courage; resolution.

Telltale, or tell-tale *noun*: 1. something that reveals information; a sign 2. somebody who tells somebody else's secrets or bad actions.

A The old man's heart told the police about the murder. So, the "heart" of the title is both a real heart and a tell-tale.

B The narrator is mad and the beating heart is in his imagination. The "heart" of the title is the "center of the narrator's sincerest feelings" that make him feel guilty.

C The old man's heart reveals his fear and so causes the murder. This is the "heart" of the title.

D The narrator is mad and hears his own heart – the muscular organ – which makes him reveal his own bad action.

3 A madman's world

In column A are the narrator's explanations for various parts of his story. In column B are more logical explanations of the same actions. Match the narrator's explanation with the more logical explanation.

A

A A disease had made the narrator's senses better than most people's.

B The careful planning of the murder shows that he was not mad.

C The narrator planned the murder in a very intelligent way.

D The narrator became excited when he heard the old man's heart.

E The policemen smiled to make fun of the narrator.

F The beating of the heart got increasingly loud.

B

1 There was no real reason to wait for seven days to murder the old man.

2 The murder of somebody who the narrator loved and with no real reason shows that he was mad.

3 The policemen felt nervous with the narrator, who was acting strangely.

4 He really heard his own heart.

5 The narrator had become mad.

6 Deep down in his unconscious, the narrator began to feel worse and worse about the murder.

4 Speaking: the hot seat

A chair in front of the class is the "hot seat". The student sitting there becomes the narrator of "The Tell-Tale Heart" or one of the policemen who finally arrested him. The other students then ask the characters questions – there are some examples below, but you can make up more. The students in the hot seat should try to make their answer correspond to the story, but obviously they will also have to invent many things.

The narrator

1 How long have you known the old man?
2 What exactly is your relationship to the old man? Is he your father? Employer? Friend?
3 Generally, if you kill somebody because of their eye, you are considered mad. Don't you agree?
4 What disease did you have?
5 You said that you saw things in heaven and hell? What things?
6 During the nights before you killed the old man, did you have any doubts about what you were doing?
7 What did the police say when they saw parts of the old man's body under the floor?
8 You have murdered somebody and now you will be executed. Do you think that is fair?

A policeman

1 When you went to the old man's house did you think anything bad had happened?
2 What was the old man like?
3 When did you first think that maybe something bad had happened to the old man?
4 In your experience, is it unusual for a murderer to feel such terrible guilt for a crime?
5 Were you shocked when you discovered the truth?
6 The murderer thinks he was very intelligent in the way he planned the murder. What do you think?

INTERNET PROJECT

"Tell-Tale Heart" at the movies

Poe's tales and poems have attracted many famous actors, and "The Tell-Tale Heart" is no exception. To see two excellent performances of this story go to www.blackcat-cideb.com. Insert the title or part of the title of the book into our search engine. Open the page for *American Horror*. Click on the Internet project links.

Present a short review of these films to your class. Say

- who the actor is
- how the story is presented
- which one you preferred and why.

Poe's poetry of horror and sadness

Poe's horror stories are much loved, but so are his poems.To find out more about his poems connect to the Internet and go to www.blackcat-cideb.com. Insert the title or part of the title of the book into our search engine. Open the page for *American Horror*. Click on the Internet project links.

Listen to some readings of these four poems: "The Raven", "The Bells", "Annabel Lee" and "Alone".

Present a short report to the class about Poe's poetry. Say:

- the names of some other of his famous poems
- some characteristics of his poems
- what some Poe's ideas on poetry were.

Then read a couple of stanzas from the poem that you like best.

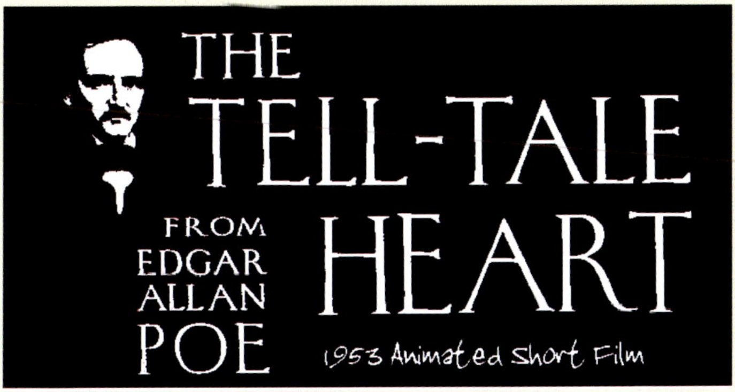

Poe's America

When Edgar Allan Poe was born in 1809, the United States of America was only 23 years old. The young country faced many problems. Not many Americans citizens felt confident that their new country could survive. First the United States had to avoid open confrontation with the two great powers of the age, France and England. This, however, was impossible because France and England were at war and United States had to side with France and England becoming the enemy of the other. This tense situation led to the War of 1812 between America and Britain.

America won this war, and their victory helped increase the young nation's self-confidence. Americans also gained confidence as they gained territory. In 1803, the United States bought 2.1 million sq km of land west of the Mississippi River from France for $15 million. When Poe was a young man it was a common belief among the American people that God wanted white Americans to possess the entire continent, or as the journalist John L. O'Sullivan wrote, it was "our manifest destiny". In fact, during Poe's life time, the United States obtained almost all its present-day territory. America's belief in Manifest Destiny was so strong that it did not hesitate to take lands away from other peoples and nations. First, the lands of the various Native American nations were taken, and then some lands of Mexico in 1845.

America's economic growth was as incredible as its territorial expansion. In the 1820s, the northern states stopped being colonial areas – or, in other words, territories that exported raw goods to England and Europe and imported manufactured goods. The Industrial Revolution and commercial agriculture had begun in America. Now American towns and cities produced the goods which American farmers bought, and those same farmers cultivated the land and raised animals to feed

American Progress, by John Gast, 1872.
Allegorical female figure of America leading pioneers and railroads westward.

themselves and the cities. During these same years, the urban population started growing faster than the rural population.

Politics also changed enormously. At this time, all white American males obtained the right to vote. The number of voters increased greatly – from 1.2 million in 1828 to 2.4 million in 1840. General Andrew Jackson, the hero of the War of 1812 and wars against Native Americans in the south, dominated the politics of this period. He ran for president as "a man of the people"

It is not difficult to see why both the Americans themselves and the Europeans were amazed. This new nation had no precedents in history. It was the first true democracy in the modern world, and after the French Revolution, it was clear to many that democracy was the way of the future.

Obviously, American writers wanted to somehow communicate the greatness of their young country in poems and novels. In 1837, the American poet and philosopher Ralph Waldo Emerson (1803-1882) gave a pubblic reading of his essay called "The American Scholar" – this was America's literary declaration of independence. Emerson

Ralph Waldo Emerson.

wrote that now, "We will walk on our own feet; we will work with our own hands; we will speak our minds." Also, America itself had become an obsession, an immense modern myth. And soon, with the novelists Herman Melville (1819-1891) and Nathaniel Hawthorne (1804-1864) and the poet Walt Whitman (1819-1892), America had its first great writers.

Like Hawthorne and Melville, Poe wrote about the dark side of the new American dream of greatness and power. Now, historians can tell us all the reasons why it was almost inevitable that the United States became a world power. However, when Poe was alive, it was not at all clear. Could a democracy, or even a monarchy, govern such a huge territory filled with so many different kinds of people?

Americans had a hard time understanding and interpreting this new world. In Europe people knew exactly where they belonged – in which social group, in which profession. After all, their families had often lived in the same place for many generations. In America these social groups no longer existed.

Many of Poe's stories record the loneliness of the new Americans, and their desperate attempt to interpret their frightening new world. Understanding and interpretation are essential for Poe's characters: if they don't succeed, they either go mad or die.

Poe described his last madman in a poem of 1849, the year he died. This madman is a knight who is looking for Eldorado – the city of gold that the Spanish Conquistadors wanted to find. This knight grows old looking for his city which is located "over the mountains of the moon". One year before Poe wrote this poem, prospectors had discovered gold in California. From 1848 to 1855 about 300,000 people crossed the continent hoping to find their own city of gold. Before the discovery of gold in 1848, San Francisco was a small village; just ten years later it was the fifteenth largest city in America. Madness or the new American dream?

1 Comprehension check

Say whether the following statements are true (T), or false (F), and then correct the false ones.

		T	F
1	The United States was a powerful country when Poe was born.	☐	☐
2	The United States bought an enormous amount of land at the beginning of the 1800s.	☐	☐
3	"Manifest Destiny" was the belief that God wanted the United States to take control of all of North America except Mexico and Canada.	☐	☐
4	The United States stole land from other peoples.	☐	☐
5	Poe lived in a period of great economic difficulty.	☐	☐
6	More and more people became involved in the democratic process during Poe's life.	☐	☐
7	Andrew Jackson, the seventh President of the United States, was a war hero.	☐	☐
8	America's first great writers after Poe were born in the late 1800s.	☐	☐
9	Poe often wrote about the optimism of the young American nation.	☐	☐
10	Poe wrote a poem about the discovery of gold and the dream of becoming rich in California.	☐	☐

1 Picture summary

A Look at the pictures from *American Horror*. Label them according to which story they are from (A-D) and the order in which they appear in that story (1, 2).

A "The Pit and the Pendulum"

B "The Facts in the Case of M. Valdemar"

C "The Black Cat"

D "The Oval Portrait"

E "The Tell-Tale Heart"

B **Work in pairs. Describe who the people in the pictures are and what is happening in each scene. Then use the pictures to give a summary of each story.**

2 Characters

Say for which of the characters each of the statements below is true. You can use the characters more than once.

PP: narrator of "The Pit and the Pendulum"

MV: narrator of "The Facts in the Case of M. Valdemar"

BC: narrator of "The Black Cat"

OP: the painter in "The Oval Portrait"

TTH: the narrator in "The Tell-Tale Heart"

1 He loved art more than he loved life.
2 He was obsessed by a physical defect.
3 He was an expert in hypnosis.
4 A French general saved him.
5 He used rats to help him escape death.
6 He did not notice that the person who loved him most in the world was dying for him.
7 He thought that he had incredible hearing.
8 He blamed alcohol for his terrible actions.
9 He left a scientifically accurate description of his frightening experiences which was also confirmed by expert witnesses.
10 His feeling of guilt caused him to be arrested by the police.
11 He was horrified by the results of his own experiments.
12 He thought he was buried alive.
13 As a child, he was very kind to animals.
14 He killed a man who was his friend.
15 He believed that the "Spirit of Perverseness" caused him to do horrible things.
16 He succeeded in stopping death.
17 He believed that there might be a supernatural explanation for what happened to him.
18 He was cruelly tormented by Spanish monks.

3 Reading pictures

Match each picture with the sentences on page 111. There are four sentences that you do not need to use.

A

B

C

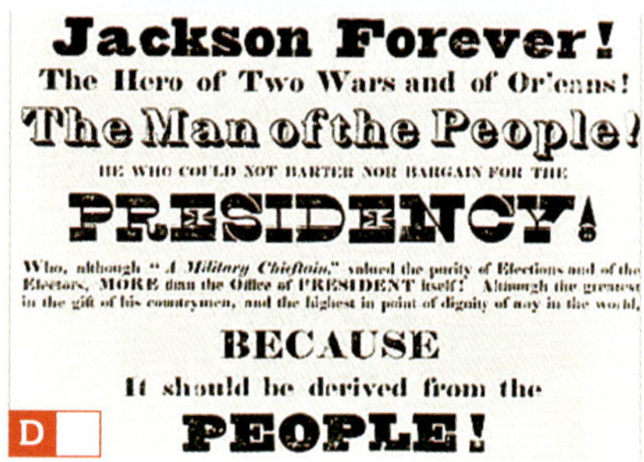

D

E

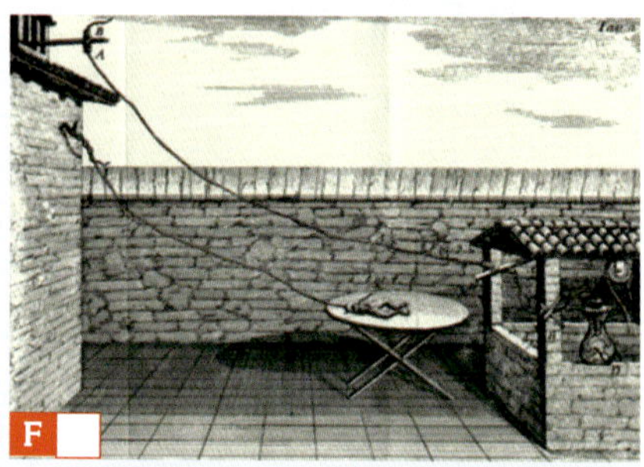

F

G

H

I

J

1 The late 1700s was the first time in history when people thought that science could change the world.

2 When Poe was alive, people started believing that scientists could defeat death and create life.

3 Edgar Allan Poe has become a popular American cultural icon.

4 During Poe's lifetime, modern democracy was born.

5 The Internet and virtual worlds are very common in science fiction nowadays.

6 Many of Poe's stories talk about worlds that only exist on computers.

7 Poe is no longer very popular in the United States.

8 Besides writing, Poe did many scientific experiments.

9 Many directors have made films based on Poe's stories and poems.

10 Poe's stories and poems often talk about real historical events and situations.

11 Real space travel in the 1960s inspired television and cinema.

12 Poe, like a number of famous rock stars and Romantic poets, is often seen as the typical tormented genius who died young.

13 Poe wanted his stories to be popular with the general reading public.

14 When Poe's stories first appeared, they were only appreciated by intellectuals.

This reader uses the **EXPANSIVE READING** approach, where the text becomes a springboard to improve language skills and to explore historical background, cultural connections and other topics suggested by the text.

The new structures introduced in this step of our **R**EADING & **T**RAINING series are listed below. Naturally, structures from lower steps are included too. For a complete list of structures used over all the six steps, see *The Black Cat Guide to Graded Readers*, which is also downloadable at no cost from our website, www.blackcat-cideb.com.

The vocabulary used at each step is carefully checked against vocabulary lists used for internationally recognised examinations.

Step **Four B2.1**

All the structures used in the previous levels, plus the following:

Verb tenses

Present Perfect Simple: *the first / second* etc. *time that ...*

Present Perfect Continuous: unfinished past with *for* or *since* (duration form)

Verb forms and patterns

Passive forms: Present Perfect Simple

Reported speech introduced by precise reporting verbs (e.g. *suggest*, *promise*, *apologise*)

Modal verbs

Be / get used to + *-ing*: habit formation

Had better: duty and warning

Types of clause

3rd Conditional: *if* + Past Perfect, *would(n't) have*

Conditionals with *may / might*

Non-defining relative clauses with: *which*, *whose*

Clauses of concession: *even though*; *in spite of*; *despite*